RAMESSES II

Other titles in the
RULERS OF THE ANCIENT WORLD series:

ALEXANDER THE GREAT
**Conqueror of
the Ancient World**
0-7660-2560-8

CLEOPATRA
Queen of Ancient Egypt
0-7660-2559-4

HANNIBAL
**Great General
of the Ancient World**
0-7660-2564-0

JULIUS CAESAR
**Ruler of
the Roman World**
0-7660-2563-2

PERICLES
**Great Leader
of Ancient Athens**
0-7660-2561-6

RAMESSES II

Ruler of Ancient Egypt

Don Nardo

Enslow Publishers, Inc.
40 Industrial Road
Box 398
Berkeley Heights, NJ 07922
USA
http://www.enslow.com

Library of Congress Cataloging-in-Publication Data

Nardo, Don, 1947-
    Ramesses II : ruler of ancient Egypt / Don Nardo.
       p. cm. — (Rulers of the ancient world)
    Includes bibliographical references and index.
    ISBN 0-7660-2562-4
    1. Egypt—History—Nineteenth dynasty, ca. 1320-1200 B.C.—Juvenile literature. 2. Ramses
II, King of Egypt—Juvenile literature. I. Title. II. Title: Ramesses the Second. III. Series.
    DT88.N37 2006
    932'.014'092—dc22

                             2005024254

Printed in the United States of America

10 9 8 7 6 5 4 3 2 1

To Our Readers:
We have done our best to make sure all Internet addresses in this book were active and appropriate
when we went to press. However, the author and the publisher have no control over and assume no
liability for the material available on those Internet sites or on other Web sites they may link to. Any
comments or suggestions can be sent by e-mail to comments@enslow.com or to the address on the
back cover.

Publisher's Note: The name of Ramesses II is spelled many ways. The two spellings that are most
used are "Ramesses" and "Ramses." While "Ramses" is most often used, most of the historians
who Enslow Publishers, Inc., consulted have indicated that "Ramesses" is the best spelling for
scholarly work. It is that spelling that we have elected to use in the text; however, within quotes and
in some book titles in the chapter notes, other spellings may be used.

CONTENTS

AN ENEMY TRAP

As near as modern historians can tell, it was in the spring of the year 1274 B.C. that one of history's greatest battles took place in southern Syria. Neither of the opposing armies was native to the area. On one side were the Egyptians, led by their pharaoh (king), Ramesses II. The region of Syria and Palestine, situated northeast of Egypt, had long been controlled by the Egyptians. And Ramesses was determined not to allow what he viewed as intruders to extend their influence into the area.

These intruders were the Hittites, led by their king, Muwatallis. The Hittites' homeland of Hatti, which the Egyptians called Kheta, was centered in Asia Minor (what is now Turkey). The rulers of Hatti were eager to keep Syria-Palestine as part of their growing empire. To this end, Muwatallis marched more than forty thousand troops into the area. This may have been one of the biggest armies ever assembled anywhere in the world up until that time.

THE TRAP

In fact, the Hittite army was nearly twice the size of the one Ramesses commanded. But the pharaoh was unaware of the enemy's strength as his own forces approached the walled town of Kadesh, near the Orontes River, in southern Syria. Ramesses did not know that a large Hittite host was waiting for him there.

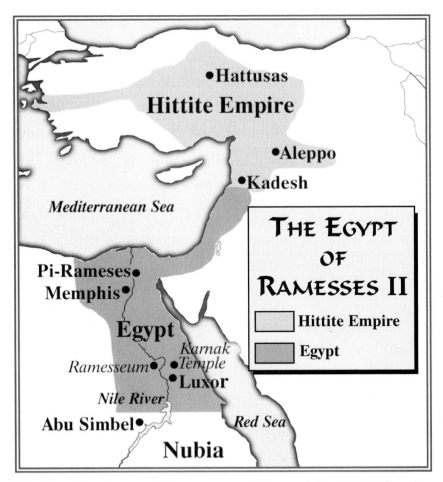

The Egyptian forces of Ramesses and those of the Hittite Empire clashed at Kadesh, near the border of the two empires.

Perhaps that is why he observed some recently adopted customs relating to Egyptian armies on the march.

One of these customs was to divide the main army into four or five smaller units. Each marched by itself, separated from the others by several miles. Ramesses commanded the unit known as Amun (named for Egypt's chief god). Meanwhile, the units Ra, Ptah, and Seth (also named for gods) lagged far behind. The plan was for all the units to meet and make camp at Kadesh. The town was then to become a base of operations in the war.

Certainly Ramesses would not have divided his forces in the usual manner if he had known how close the Hittite army was. In this regard, Muwatallis had proved himself a clever strategist. Intending to lay a trap for the Egyptians, the Hittite ruler placed most of his troops on the northwest side of Kadesh. That way, Ramesses' scouts, who were approaching from the southeast, would not be able to see them. According to one of the later Egyptian accounts of these events:

> The despicable [bad] ruler of Hatti stood amidst the army which was with him. He could not come out to fight for fear of His Majesty [Ramesses], so he sent out men and chariotry [groups of chariots], abundant, exceedingly numerous like the sand, they being three men to a chariot . . . and being armed with every kind of a weapon of war. See, they had been made to stand behind the town of Kadesh. . . . Meanwhile, His Majesty was established on the north [side] of the town of Kadesh, on the west side of the Orontes [River].[1]

The last part of this inscription—the claim that Muwatallis was afraid to fight Ramesses—was probably pure Egyptian propaganda. More likely, the Hittite king was merely biding his time, waiting for the right moment to strike.

THE DOUBLE AGENTS

In the meantime, it was very important to Muwatallis that his opponent fall into the trap. The best way to accomplish this, the Hittite ruler reasoned, was to make Ramesses think the opposing army was far away to the north. To create this ruse, Muwatallis enlisted the aid of two local men. At his bidding, they approached Ramesses while the pharaoh was camped near Shabtuna, a town not far south of Kadesh. These men pretended that they wanted to help Ramesses. But in reality they were double agents and the message they carried was false. One Egyptian account gave the message as follows:

> It is our brothers, who are tribal chiefs with the [king] of Hatti who have sent us to His Majesty [Ramesses], saying, "We shall become servants of Pharaoh, and we shall separate ourselves from the ruler of Hatti." Then said His Majesty to them, "Who are they, your brothers, who sent you to speak of this matter?". . . Then they said . . . "They are where the despicable chief of Hatti is, for [he] is in the land of Aleppo, to the north of Tunip [located many miles north of Kadesh]. He feared [the armed might] of Pharaoh too much [and refuses] to come southward.". . . Now these [men] said these things

THE HITTITE ARMY GATHERS STRENGTH

This is a surviving Egyptian account (translated by Kenneth Kitchen in his *Ramesside Inscriptions*) from the period of Ramesses' major Kadesh campaign. Clearly biased in favor of the Egyptian viewpoint, it tells how the Hittite king, Muwatallis (referred to in the account as "the fallen chief of Hatti") gathered military forces from many Near Eastern peoples who were then subjects or allies of the Hittites.

> The despicable fallen chief of Hatti had come [to Kadesh]. He had gathered round himself all foreign countries to the farthest limits of the [Mediterranean] sea. The entire land of Hatti had come, [and many other lands]. . . . He left not even one country which was not brought [with him to Kadesh], of every distant land. Their rulers were there with him, each man with his [military] forces. Their chariotry was vast in extent, [and] unequalled. [There were so many troops that] they covered every hill and valley. They were like the locust swarm in their multitude.[2]

Ramesses II

to His Majesty so as to prevent His Majesty's army from being prepared to fight.[3]

At this point, Ramesses faced a sticky problem, one that military commanders have had to wrestle with throughout recorded history. Namely, should he trust a seemingly vital piece of military intelligence that had come his way? If the men were lying, he knew it could spell disaster for the Egyptians. But there seemed to be no reason to doubt the truth of their claims. After all, thus far there had been no sign of the Hittite army in the Kadesh region. Vanity may also have played a role in the pharaoh's decision. The personal boasts and claims Ramesses made in many of his carved inscriptions show how he viewed himself. He saw himself as a mighty war leader like his recently deceased father, King Seti I. So it probably flattered Ramesses' ego to think that his enemy feared meeting him in open battle.

Perhaps these were the reasons that Ramesses eventually accepted the story told by the double agents. Whatever motivated the pharaoh's decision, he took the bait and led the troops of Amun across the Orontes River. They then moved onto the level plain that stretched before Kadesh. Soon the town, with its high defensive walls, became plainly visible in the distance. All seemed quiet, so the pharaoh ordered his men to make camp. The soldiers of the Ra, Ptah, and Seth units would join them in the next day or so, he said. And then the whole army would lay siege to the city. This was necessary because Kadesh had recently switched its allegiance from Egypt to Hatti.

THE CAPTURED SPIES

At this point, Ramesses still had no idea that his enemy, Muwatallis, was waiting with a huge army on the far side of the city. Fortunately for the Egyptians, however, the pharaoh did not completely relax his guard. Following another custom of military campaigns, he sent out some scouts to survey the area near the town. It was also lucky for Ramesses that these scouts were excellent trackers and brave soldiers. While on patrol, they detected the presence of two Hittite scouts—their enemy counterparts. The Egyptians ambushed and captured these men.

Ramesses was sitting on a gold-plated throne in his command tent when one of his aides told him about the captured spies. He immediately ordered that they be brought before him. At first, the men refused to admit who they were and why they had been lurking in the area. So Ramesses ordered that they be beaten until they told the truth. The spies soon began to talk.

"What [i.e., who] are you?" the pharaoh demanded (according to an official Egyptian account). One of the men answered, "We belong to the ruler of Hatti. He it is who sent us to see where His Majesty [Ramesses] is [and to spy on the Egyptian army]." Then Ramesses asked, "Where is he himself, the ruler of Hatti? See, I have heard that he is in the land of Aleppo, to the north of Tunip." Reluctantly, the spies admitted that this was not the case. They told Ramesses:

> See, the despicable ruler of Hatti [Muwatallis] has already come [here], along with the [troops of] many foreign lands that accompany him, whom he has brought

with him as allies. . . . They are furnished with their infantry and chariotry . . . [and] they are more numerous than the sands of the seashore. See, they stand equipped, ready to fight, behind old Kadesh![4]

Ramesses had to be disturbed, even alarmed, to hear that the enemy forces were both near and prepared for battle. He immediately dispatched runners toward the south to warn the Ra, Ptah, and Seth units of the impending danger. For the Ra division, it was already too late.

The men of Ra had just crossed the Orontes. Unprepared for battle, they were moving leisurely across the plain, some in their chariots, but most on foot. Ptah and Seth were still many miles behind.

THE SNEAK ATTACK

This was the moment for which Muwatallis had been waiting. He ordered a large number of his chariots to move out from their hiding place behind the town and attack Ra on one of its unprotected sides. For the men of Ra, the first sign of the oncoming assault was probably a large cloud of dust kicked up by the Hittite horses. Then, suddenly, out of the cloud emerged thousands of chariots charging at full speed. Completely unprepared for battle, the Egyptians fell into confusion. Their own chariots, lighter than the enemy's and far fewer in number, were smashed or swept aside. It was as if they were stalks of wheat sliced in half by a huge sickle. Having inflicted this damage, some of the Hittite vehicles turned and charged again.

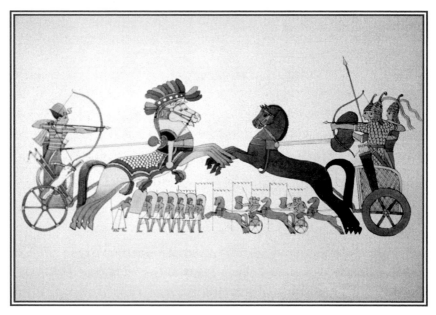

The battle between the Egyptian and Hittite forces at Kadesh was fierce as chariots charged and soldiers clashed amid swirling dust.

Meanwhile, most of Ra's infantrymen (foot soldiers) fled northward. Evidently they hoped to find the pharaoh's camp and the safety it might afford them. This security turned out to be more imagined than real. When the troops of Amun saw the men of Ra running toward them with the Hittites in close pursuit, the Amun camp, as Ra had, fell into a state of chaos.

Ramesses' guards and aides alerted him to the oncoming danger. But like everyone else in camp, he had precious little time to prepare. The first priority was to protect his person, so he swiftly prepared for battle. One of his official accounts of the event states:

> Then His Majesty [Ramesses] appeared gloriously . . .
> took his panoply of war [complete array of armor], and

girded [prepared] himself in his coat of mail [armor]. . . .
The great chariot which bore His Majesty was named
Victory in Thebes.[5]

Ramesses was also concerned for his splintered
army and the possibility that it would quickly suffer a
terrible defeat. He realized that he must set an example
for his terrified men. He must urge them to rally around
their royal leader. "Then His Majesty [Ramesses] set
forth at the gallop," the official account continues:

> He plunged into the midst of the forces of the Hittite
> foe, he being entirely on his own, [and having] no one
> else with him [to protect him]. [Looking around himself]
> he found 2,500 [enemy] chariots hemming him in, all
> around him.[6]

The surviving accounts say that Ramesses rode out
to meet the enemy, likely accompanied only by his
personal bodyguards. It was an act of raw courage and
desperation. The young pharaoh knew full well that this
was his moment of truth, a turning point that would
decide not only his own fate, but that of his country. The
question was whether his troops would rally to his side.
Even if they did, there was no guarantee that they would
be able to turn the tide of battle in their favor. But it was
clear that if they did not regroup and come to his aid, all
would be lost.

2

RISE TO
THE THRONE

The people of Egypt remembered Ramesses II for many centuries after his long reign (ca. 1279–1213 B.C.). To them, he was one of their greatest pharaohs, if not *the* greatest. Most modern historians agree that this was not an exaggerated judgment. Indeed, Ramesses' reign was not only very long when compared to the reigns of most other Egyptian pharaohs; his years on the throne were also filled with energetic activities of all kinds. These included huge construction projects and an ambitious foreign policy that involved numerous military expeditions into nearby lands. The giant statues and splendid temples he erected survived over the years. These monuments awed later generations of Egyptians and continue to amaze and fascinate people today. He was also a key player in the first great battle recorded in history, a conflict that decided the fate of Egypt for centuries to come.

Thanks to Ramesses' larger-than-life achievements, his name far outlived him, his children, and even his great-grandchildren. Memories of his deeds persisted in the monuments and written records he left behind. As a result, long after most other Egyptian pharaohs had been forgotten, the name and legend of Ramesses II remained. They lived on, fixed in the cultural memory of peoples across the Near East, Europe, and beyond.

TRYING TO RECONSTRUCT THE REAL RAMESSES

Like so many other people down through the ages, modern scholars have been fascinated with Ramesses' legend. But the very fact that he and his accomplishments became legendary presents certain problems for those who seek to reconstruct the past. Separating the real person from the legend is often a very difficult task. This is especially true in the case of the Egyptian pharaohs. They generally did not leave behind factual, objective summaries of their deeds. And there were no newspapers or other independent media in those days to record the real facts for posterity.

Instead, the Egyptian kings, including Ramesses, had artists and writers (scribes) create official records of their deeds. These records—consisting of texts, paintings, and reliefs (scenes carved on walls)—were a kind of propaganda. They were intended to glorify the king, impress his subjects, and thereby ensure his continued power. Although these records usually contained elements of truth, they exaggerated the pharaohs' positive traits. They also glossed over or omitted their mistakes or defeats. So modern historians do not take these biased accounts literally and must be careful in interpreting them.

How, then, do historians know enough about the real Ramesses to write an objective biography of him? First, they look at the archaeological remains of his temples, palaces, and statues. These reveal what Ramesses looked like and the general physical conditions in which he lived. Second, they look at the surviving evidence about his parents, wives, and children. They also look at the government administrators who worked for him. This reveals a fair amount about his character, habits, and likes and dislikes. Also revealing are non-Egyptian sources that mention Ramesses, such as a treaty he signed with the king of a foreign land. In addition, modern investigators have examined Ramesses' tomb and mummy, which were uncovered in the nineteenth century.

A PRODUCT OF HIS HERITAGE

In telling the story of Ramesses' eventful life, one must take into account all of these diverse sources. But the story must begin well before he was born, however. This is because Ramesses was, like every other person who has ever lived, partially a product of his heritage. Customs and culture had been established in his region well before he was born.

For example, Ramesses' view of his country and the place it occupied in the world was shaped in large part by centuries of Egyptian tradition. Long before his birth, the people of Egypt had come to see themselves in a certain way. They had developed an exaggerated sense of their own importance in the world. This was largely the result of Egypt's unusual geography. Most Egyptians lived on a narrow, fertile strip of land running north-to-south along either side of the Nile River. Beyond this habitable region were many miles of dry deserts.

Before Ramesses' time, including during the Old Kingdom (ca. 2686–2181 B.C.), these wastelands had played a key role in Egypt. They had more or less isolated, and also insulated (protected), the Egyptians from the outside world. Over time, the Egyptians had come to believe that they dwelled in the very center of creation. This gave them a sense of independence and natural superiority. In this way, noted historian Lionel Casson points out, Egypt's geography

> assured the society that arose there an infancy snug and secure, unaffected by what went on in the regions round about. On three sides deserts formed a barrier, and on the fourth, the sea. . . . In Upper Egypt the sun shone all day all year, while lower Egypt received hardly more than a touch of rain. The Egyptians were blessedly ignorant of the violent weather that caused [the inhabitants of] Mesopotamia to make the god of storm their chief deity. . . . They conceived of the world as stable and benign, and it is easy to see why, in their isolation and security, they did so.[1]

This sense of isolation eventually faded as the Egyptians made increasing contacts with other lands. By the time of Ramesses' own era, encompassing much of the thirteenth century B.C., Egypt was far more

21

connected to the surrounding world. Egyptians had seen the need for contact with its neighboring nations and kingdoms. For the Egyptians, Casson says, this situation

> was a far cry from the insular [isolated and protected] days of the Old Kingdom. The pharaoh maintained diplomatic relations with rulers in Crete [an island off the coast of Greece], Asia Minor, Cyprus [an island south of Asia Minor], and Palestine, and his agents traded with all these places. There were Libyan, Sudanese, and Asia Minor units in the [Egyptian] army. Nobles were served by slaves brought from foreign lands. Egypt became richer, more powerful, more flexible, and varied.[2]

Thus, Ramesses was born in an age in which Egypt had ongoing diplomatic relations and trade with other nations. Egypt also possessed the potential for expansion by conquest, a policy Ramesses would exploit more than many of his predecessors had.

IN THE SHADOW OF HIS PREDECESSORS

Ramesses' social position and opportunities for political authority and power were also largely shaped by events that occurred before he was born. He and his immediate predecessors on the throne ruled in an era that modern scholars call the New Kingdom. The word "new" suggests that Egypt boasted a long and proud heritage before the advent of the New Kingdom. The Egyptian nation had been founded by the first pharaoh, Menes, in about 3100 B.C. Later, in the Old Kingdom, several pharaohs erected huge stone monuments, including the great pyramids at Giza (near modern-day Cairo). In the Middle Kingdom (ca. 2055–1650 B.C.), Egypt began to expand its influence outward through trade with other lands.

Then, in 1650 B.C., a foreign people, the Hyksos, invaded Egypt. They occupied much of the country for a century. The Egyptians were humbled and humiliated, but they eventually rallied and struck back under a pharaoh named Ahmose. The defeat of the Hyksos, circa 1550 B.C., marked the beginning of the glorious New Kingdom. This was an era characterized by a long line of warrior pharaohs. They launched military campaigns and conquered lands beyond Egypt's borders, creating an empire. Ramesses was a member of this line of vigorous rulers. In a very real sense, he stood in their huge shadows. And he was proud to perpetuate their vision of Egypt as the cultural and military superpower of the known world.

But there was another dimension to Ramesses' royal heritage. It inevitably affected his image, goals, and the nature of his achievements. Most of the New Kingdom pharaohs had been born into noble or royal families. In 1323 B.C., however, the throne was occupied by Horemheb, a former career military officer who had risen to the rank of general. Horemheb had no son to carry on his royal line. So he chose a man very much like himself to succeed him.

This man, a former soldier named Ramesses, became pharaoh when Horemheb died in 1295 B.C. Unlike Horemheb, however, King Ramesses I already had both a son, Seti, and a grandson, also named Ramesses. When Ramesses I died in 1294 B.C. after ruling for only a year, Seti became king. And Seti's son eventually succeeded him on the throne as Ramesses II.

Thus, a new dynasty (family line of rulers) began with Ramesses I. (Modern scholars number it as Egypt's Nineteenth Dynasty, lasting from 1295 to 1186 B.C.) Of the eight rulers of this dynasty, Seti and his son, Ramesses, were by far the most accomplished. Their exploits on the battlefield and the numerous structures they erected brought them fame and glory while they lived. The legacies they left behind dwarfed those of most of the pharaohs who came before and after them.

 ## GROOMED BY HIS FATHER

Indeed, Ramesses' own goals and accomplishments as pharaoh were closely tied to those of his father. In fact, the evidence suggests that Seti began carefully grooming his son for the throne when the boy was very young. Seti was in his thirties when he succeeded his own father as pharaoh. At that time, Seti's wife, Mut-Tuya, had already given him three children. The first, a boy, had died in infancy. But a girl named Tia and a second son, Ramesses, had survived and were perhaps ten and eight years old, respectively, when Seti became pharaoh.

On reaching the throne, Seti immediately began setting a strong example for his son. The new pharaoh purposely chose the same regal titles (customary extra names taken by each king) used by two of the greatest rulers of the preceding dynasty (the Eighteenth). Seti

RAMESSES' MANY NAMES

History remembers the son of King Seti I as Ramesses II. However, Ramesses was only one of several names by which this pharaoh identified himself. In fact, during the New Kingdom each pharaoh took at least five names. Ramesses was this pharaoh's nomen, or personal name, the one he received at birth. His praenomen, or formal throne name, was Usermaatre (meaning "Strong in the Truth of Ra"). All official correspondence, including letters to and from foreign rulers, used his praenomen. By custom, a pharaoh's nomen and praenomen were written in a pair of cartouches, small oval-shaped plaques or painted symbols that identified him or her.

Egyptian kings also had various honorary names, usually taking the form of descriptive, often flowery phrases. One was the Horus name, which linked a king to the god Horus, son of Osiris (lord of the Underworld and bringer of yearly renewal). Ramesses' Horus name was "Strong Bull, Beloved of Right and Truth." His other names included "Protector of Egypt Who Curbs the Foreign Lands," and "Rich in Years, Great in Victories."

called himself "Strong Bull Appearing in Thebes" after the great warrior-pharaoh Thutmose III. Seti I also took the name "Heir of Ra" after the great builder Amenhotep III.

Seti launched several military campaigns into Palestine to strengthen Egypt's already considerable influence in that area. During these expeditions he secured the Mediterranean ports of Tyre, Sidon, Byblos, and Simyra. This ensured that Egypt could continue to import supplies of timber and other valuable goods from the region. But more important, Seti's aggressive moves in Palestine were part of an overall strategy designed to control the region. First, Seti felt it crucial to counter the influence of the Hittites, who had made their own claims on Palestine. Second, both nations wanted to control or at least have access to valuable trade routes that ran through the area. By launching military expeditions, Seti hoped to ensure that Egypt could continue to benefit from international trade.

At first, apparently, the pharaoh felt that Ramesses was too young to go along on these expeditions. However, the situation soon changed dramatically. In about 1288 B.C., when Ramesses was about fourteen, Seti led the Egyptian army westward. Tribal groups from the deserts of Libya, located along Egypt's western border, were threatening some of the settlements in the fertile Nile Delta. Seti gave Ramesses the prestigious title of "Commander-in-chief of the Army" and took him along on the campaign. In all likelihood, however, this title the young man bore was largely ceremonial. Seti still commanded the army. Nevertheless, Ramesses did play a direct role in the campaign (although the exact nature of that role is unknown). The young man also experienced his first taste of battle.

Two years later, when he was about sixteen, Ramesses accompanied his father on another military campaign. Several years before, two towns in southern Syria, Amurru and Kadesh, had fallen under the influence of the Hittites. Seti was determined to return these towns to Egypt's sphere of influence. Though they made the journey to Syria, Seti, Ramesses, and their troops never actually met the Hittites in battle. Instead, for reasons that remain unclear, they accepted an uneasy truce. Then they marched home.

RAMESSES BECOMES COREGENT

Ramesses performed capably in these campaigns. This must have convinced his father that the young man was ready for his first actual command. At some point in the late 1280s B.C., when Ramesses was about twenty, he led an expedition into Nubia. This land, populated by black Africans, was located directly south of Egypt. (At the time, most Egyptians were olive-skinned, like modern-days Arabs.) In the past, the Nubians had frequently rebelled against Egyptian influence and control. Ramesses now responded to the latest rebellion. It turned out to be a short war, for the Nubian troops quickly fled before the better-equipped and better-trained Egyptian army. Nevertheless, Ramesses viewed it as a splendid victory. He celebrated it by erecting a

CARVED DEPICTIONS OF THE SUCCESSFUL NUBIAN EXPEDITION

The temple Ramesses erected in Nubia to celebrate his successful campaign in the late 1280s B.C. contained a series of elaborate relief sculptures depicting the events of that expedition. The late, great scholar of ancient Egypt, James H. Breasted, described how Ramesses appeared in some of the carved scenes.

Ramesses, standing in his chariot with drawn bow, charges the Nubians, who flee in a horde before him into a palm grove. Two Nubians lead away a wounded comrade to his family. Behind him charge two [Nubian] prices in their chariots. On the right [in a different section of the relief] sits Ramesses enthroned. Approaching from the left are two long lines of Nubians, bringing furniture of ebony and ivory, panther hides, gold in large rings, bows, myrrh [a spice], shields, elephant tusks . . . ostrich feathers, ostrich eggs, [and] live animals, including monkeys, panthers, a giraffe . . . and an ostrich [all of these gifts meant as tribute to acknowledge Ramesses' victory].[3]

This carving from a temple at Abu Simbel shows Ramesses' victory over the Nubians.

temple whose walls bore carved reliefs of scenes from the campaign.

It appears that by this time Seti had already made Ramesses coregent, a sort of junior coruler. (The exact year this occurred is unclear.) Because of the manner in which he himself had come to the throne, Seti was well aware of how unexpected and sudden a pharaoh's death could be. He wanted the transition following his own passing to be as smooth as possible. By making Ramesses coregent, Seti ensured that his son's ascent to the throne would be quick and effortless.

Ramesses later described the coregency and Seti's motive for it in an inscription (words painted on or carved onto stone). The single longest written passage produced in Ramesses' reign, it was inscribed on a wall of Seti's mortuary temple at Abydos, situated about sixty miles northwest of the major Egyptian city of Thebes. (Mortuary temples were built in honor of the pharaohs. The priests in such a temple prayed and sacrificed to ensure the prosperity of the pharaoh's spirit in the afterlife.)

Not surprisingly, while praising his deceased father in the inscription, Ramesses also tried to inflate his own image and prestige. For example, one passage begins with the words: "I came forth from Ra you say, while Seti brought me up." Egyptian pharaohs traditionally associated themselves with the sun god, Ra. (This god was more often called Amun-Ra in the New Kingdom.) Ramesses seemed to be saying that he had two fathers—one, Ra, had given him life, while the other, Seti, had raised him. This image of Seti as the caretaker of Ramesses continues in the next few lines. "The Lord of All [Amun-Ra] himself magnified me [made me great] while I was a child, until I became ruler [of Egypt]. He assigned me to the land [of Egypt] while I was yet in the egg [i.e., in the womb]."[4]

Eventually, the inscription gets around to praising Seti's choice to make Ramesses coregent. It also describes the coregency crowning ceremony. And it directly quotes Seti, probably capturing some of the formal words said on such occasions. Ramesses wrote:

> I reported [for duty] as chief of infantry and chariotry [in the Libyan, Syrian, and Nubian campaigns]. When my father appeared to the populace . . . he spoke thus concerning me: "Crown him as king, that I may see his beauty [as a ruler] while I yet live!" [Then Seti ordered] the chamberlains [high-placed members of the royal court] to set the crown upon my brow. "Set the crown upon his head . . . He shall govern this land, he shall care for its boundaries, [and] he shall give commands to the people." [His eyes filled with] tears, so great was the love for me within him.[5]

ACCOMPLISHMENTS AS CORULER

The surviving evidence shows that when Seti made Ramesses coregent it was not intended merely for show. The pharaoh also bestowed on his son many of the privileges and powers that Seti himself enjoyed. One clear example of such a privilege involved the young man's love life. According to the Abydos inscription, "He [Seti] furnished me with a household [containing women] from the royal harem, comparable with the beauties of the [Egyptian royal] Palace. He selected for me wives [and other female companions]."[6]

Many pharaohs kept harems, including Seti. The tradition was designed in part to ensure that a pharaoh would have several sons, one of whom would end up succeeding him. (The failure to produce suitable offspring, as in Horemheb's case, was considered very undesirable.) This means that Ramesses' mother, Mut-Tuya, was Seti's chief wife rather than his only mate. Clearly, Seti expected his son to carry on the same tradition with his own group of wives and mistresses.

The abilities and performance Ramesses displayed while coregent were often impressive. It has already been established that he went on military campaigns while still in his teens. It may be that Seti gave him sole command in the Nubian expedition because the young man possessed exceptional intelligence and leadership abilities. Or it could be that Seti wanted to give his son a chance to practice his soldiering skills in an "easy" war. After all, the Egyptians had long seen the Nubians as weak and not much of a threat to Egyptian armies.

Seti apparently delegated a great deal of other authority and tasks to his son. "I commanded that his [mortuary] temple should be supplied," Ramesses wrote in the Abydos inscription. The job of building a pharaoh's mortuary temple was a major and highly prestigious assignment. Ramesses also said:

> I established his fields [that surrounded the mortuary temple, part of a temple estate]. I instituted [planted or grew] for him . . . all kinds of fruit, all kinds of fresh vegetables, and orchards growing for him. See, his temple was under my supervision, from when [I first became king].[7]

If these claims made in the inscription are true, they paint a flattering picture of the young Ramesses. They portray him as an energetic, industrious, ambitious, and highly versatile individual. He even seemed to have an

RAMESSES ADDRESSES HIS DEAD FATHER

In these excerpts from Ramesses' great inscription at Abydos (translated by Kenneth Kitchen), the newly enthroned pharaoh addresses his recently deceased father, King Seti I, and assures him that all preparations have been made for his journey in the afterlife:

> O my father, Seti, who is now a god! . . . I have devoted attention to your temple, your food offerings [to appease the gods] being assured. You [rest] in the netherworld [the afterlife], while I appear as Ra to the common people, I being on the great throne. . . . I have built the temple that you loved, your image being in it. . . . I have finished the work on it. . . . I have enriched your treasury, filled with desirable goods which I have given to you, along with your revenues. I have given you a ship carrying cargoes on the sea. . . . I have assembled your herds of all kinds of small cattle, to supply your offerings [to the gods] faithfully. See, you have entered the sky, you follow Ra [in his daily journey across the sky], you having mingled with the stars and the moon.[8]

appreciation for art and its power to glorify a ruler's image. While still a teenager, Ramesses ordered the creation of a golden statute of his father.

In spite of Ramesses' considerable powers, duties, and accomplishments as co-regent, he evidently never posed a threat to his father's rule. In ancient times it was common for rulers' next of kin to try to push the rulers aside in an effort to gain power for themselves. This was not as common in Egypt as it was elsewhere, however. Ramesses does not seem to have had any intentions of challenging his father's authority. This may have been in part because he genuinely loved and respected Seti. But it was probably also because Seti was a strong and confident ruler in his own right. Almost certainly he saw to it that as long as he was alive his son remained in a lesser role. As scholar Joyce Tyldesley points out, the coregency was not

> a partnership of equals. Even after his [crowning], when he was permitted to use his own titles . . . Ramesses was very much the junior or deputy monarch. He did not, for example, start to count his own regnal years [the consecutive years of his reign] until he became sole ruler. Now [as a youthful coregent] he devoted himself to learning his trade [i.e., the job of being pharaoh], serving as his father's deputy.[9]

All this changed when Seti died in 1279 B.C. Ramesses was now sole ruler of Egypt. (His age at this point is unclear, mainly because the date of his birth is unknown. But most scholars believe he was by then in his twenties.) The new pharaoh waited for his father's body to be properly embalmed (a process that often took from fifty to seventy days). Then Ramesses saw to it that Seti's remains were placed in a tomb that had been prepared in the Valley of the Kings. (Hoping to escape the ravages of tomb robbers, many of the New Kingdom pharaohs chose to be buried in this desolate location in the mountains near Thebes.) Seti had ruled Egypt for some fifteen years. At the time, no one could have foreseen that Ramesses' reign would last more than four times as long as his father's.

3

FAMILY AND PRIVATE LIFE

Surviving statues and inscriptions show clearly that all of Egypt's pharaohs had wives and children they cared about. But no other pharaoh before Ramesses II had as many wives and children. The exact number of his wives is unknown but surely it was at least several dozen. These women bore him a total of perhaps a hundred children. (Again, the exact number remains and will likely always be unclear.) Moreover, Ramesses frequently depicted his relatives in paintings and sculptures. This suggests that he enjoyed and took pride in his family and had a complex and rich private life.

THE QUEEN MOTHER

Next to his father, Seti, the most important relative with whom Ramesses shared a relationship was his mother, Mut-Tuya, Seti's chief wife. That Ramesses deeply loved and respected his mother is clear from her flattering images on his many monuments. He ordered that her likeness be carved permanently in stone in numerous temples and other structures.

For example, statues of Mut-Tuya are prominent at Ramesses' great temple at Abu Simbel (in Nubia, about 170 miles south of the Egyptian town of Aswan). It is significant that these statues are roughly the same size as those of the pharaoh's chief wives and leading sons. It was customary in Egyptian art to show the status and importance of relatives, associates, and others by the size of their images. The people seen as most important had the biggest statues (though with rare exceptions never as big as the king's). Meanwhile, people of lower status had successively smaller statues. The large size, as well as large number, of Mut-Tuya's images demonstrates the high regard in which her son held her.

Mut-Tuya was not of royal birth. Like Seti and Ramesses himself, she was part of a family of high-placed people who suddenly became royals when Horemheb chose Ramesses I to succeed him. Despite his mother's lack of royal blood, Ramesses II portrayed her as a grand old dame of the royal court. He also virtually rewrote her mundane background story. As depicted in his official art, Mut-Tuya had received the divine seed of the god Amun so that she could give birth to a semidivine son. She died in the twenty-second year of Ramesses' reign, by then likely in her sixties. He buried her with considerable pomp in a spacious tomb in the Valley of the Queens (located near the Valley of the Kings).

 ## THE ROYAL HAREM

Although Mut-Tuya had been Seti's favorite wife, she was only one of many in his harem. (Similarly, Ramesses'

Ramesses' Sister and Brother-in-Law

Not much of a concrete nature is known about Ramesses' sister, Tia. But enough evidence has survived to show that she remained a part of the royal court throughout a considerable portion of his reign. When she was a teenager, her father, Seti, then still pharaoh, arranged for her to marry a high-ranking civil servant. His name, coincidentally, was also Tia.

The couple continued to enjoy royal favor under Ramesses when he succeeded Seti on the throne. The male Tia went on to become overseer of the treasury of Ramesses' great mortuary temple (the Ramesseum) near Thebes. The female Tia became involved in religious activities. Among other things, she may have sung in religious processions and other temple rituals. That Ramesses cared for his sister is demonstrated by the richness of her burial. He laid her and her husband to rest in a splendid tomb equipped with a column-lined courtyard and a small pyramid.

numerous wives were part of his own harem.) A pharaoh's harem was one of the major assets or institutions of his private life. Ramesses surely spent a great deal of his time dining and sleeping with his wives and making sure they were comfortable and secure. (It is unknown whether he always dined with wives and other relatives. Also unclear is whether custom dictated the maximum number of wives he should dine with at the same time.)

Where did Ramesses' wives come from and how did he choose them? Ancient Egyptian royal harems were often family-oriented. Children were cared for, food cooked, and other household work could be done in privacy. A major goal was the production of children, especially heirs for the throne.

Moreover, the royal harem was a sort of refuge for high-placed young women who had no husbands or brothers to look after them. Among them were the unmarried and widowed daughters, sisters, and aunts of Egyptian nobles and military generals. The unwed daughters or sisters of foreign dignitaries were sometimes invited to join the harem as well. (It is unknown how many members of an Egyptian harem were invited to join in this manner.) In addition, some evidence suggests, if a new wife already had a daughter, the girl also became a royal wife when she was old enough. (Most young girls in ancient Egypt married when they were between twelve and fourteen.)

Evidence also shows that some of these wives performed various jobs within the palace. Usually a minor wife served as a maid or hairdresser for a major wife. The fact is that the women in a pharaoh's harem were decidedly unequal in wifely status, responsibilities, and privileges. They followed strict rules regarding their status. Some wives enjoyed high status, others had moderate status, and still others had fairly low status. But the only member of the harem who had the status of queen was the pharaoh's principal wife. This allowed her to accompany him when he performed various rituals in religious temples. Thus, says Gay Robins, a noted scholar of ancient Egyptian women:

> Ritually, [she] was the most important of the royal [wives], and [she] was singled out from the rest by her insignia [special clothes, jewelry, and so on], titles, and the contexts in which [she] was depicted. . . . Queens appear most frequently in scenes from temples or on royal stelae [stones bearing painted or carved messages], following the king, who performs a ritual action. . . . Normally queens are inactive in these scenes, but they may offer [gifts] to a deity or shake a sistrum [a rattle-like musical instrument]. It is possible that a queen actually took part in some rituals.[1]

One question that naturally arises is just how high the status of a royal wife could go. Could a queen attain or claim semi-divine status, as her husband could? The answer seems to be yes, although within certain limits. It was thought that no matter how humble a royal wife's origins might be, she could not help but be touched by divinity. In other words, after she had become a pharaoh's spouse and borne his children, at least a little bit of his divinity was bound to rub off on her. Following this reasoning, several New Kingdom pharaohs endowed their chief wives with titles, crowns, tombs, and even temples. In the eyes of the Egyptian people, this linked these women to various goddesses.

AN IMPERISHABLE RECORD OF AFFECTION

Ramesses' chief wife, Nefertari, was a case in point. It remains unknown who she was before she married the man many came to see as Egypt's greatest pharaoh. But archaeologists have found an interesting clue. When they excavated her tomb, they found a small knob that came from a walking stick. The knob bears the name of Ay, the pharaoh whom Horemheb had succeeded on the throne circa 1323 B.C. This discovery raises the possibility that Nefertari was granddaughter, niece, or perhaps great-niece of Ay's.

For his own reasons, Ramesses raised Nefertari to the high status of chief wife. She remained in this position until her death. Among other important titles, he gave her the honorary name "Beloved of Mut." Mut was a vulture-goddess thought to be the chief consort of Amun-Ra and therefore highly respected in Egypt.

Tradition and politics may well have been part of why Ramesses' gave Nefertari her various honorary titles. But there is sufficient evidence to suggest that true love was another factor. It might even have been the main factor. Numerous paintings, statues, and inscriptions Ramesses left behind on many of his buildings seem to indicate that he deeply loved Nefertari. These signs were found in particularly large numbers at his

This wall painting of Queen Nefertari appears in the tomb built for her by Ramesses in Luxor, Egypt.

great temple at Abu Simbel. Ramesses also built Nefertari her own temple near his at Abu Simbel (although hers is considerably smaller than his).

Another reason for the closeness of the king and queen was undoubtedly the fact that she bore him his eldest son—Prince Amunhirwenemef. The boy was born to the couple when Ramesses was still coregent under Seti. Nefertari gave Ramesses four other sons, plus two daughters—Meritamun and Meritatum.

Given these facts about Nefertari, Ramesses must have been devastated when she died in the twenty-fourth year of his reign. She was likely only in her thirties at the time. The cause of death is unknown. The king buried her in splendor in a tomb in the Valley of the Queens. That tomb (which modern scholars named QV 66), was discovered in 1904 by Italian archaeologists. It had been looted of all its valuables in ancient times. But the walls and ceilings of the chambers still retained a series of magnificent paintings. Worthy of a pharaoh, these works testify to the high degree of love and respect Ramesses had for Nefertari.

RAMESSES' OTHER WIVES

Nefertari's untimely death left Ramesses with a problem. Namely, he now had no principal royal wife and chief consort. He greatly missed Nefertari and grieved for her. However, longstanding political and social customs demanded that he replace her. To make the selection he quite naturally turned to his harem. One of his favorite wives (after Nefertari, of course) was a woman named

RAMESSES' FAVORITE WIFE

The great modern Egyptian archaeologist, Zahi Hawass, an authority on Ramesses and his building projects, here describes the pharaoh's chief and most beloved wife—Nefertari—and the temple Ramesses erected in her honor at Abu Simbel.

> The monuments of Queen Nefertari suggest that she was a very beautiful woman. . . . During the first twenty years of his reign, her statues were often placed side by side with his. He built a tomb for her . . . which remains one of the most beautiful and famous of [Egyptian] tombs. . . . Nefertari had many titles that show not only her official standing [in the harem and the royal court], but also the love and esteem that her husband had for her. She was the "lady of Upper and Lower Egypt and the Delta," "Lady of All lands," "The Greatly Praised one," "The Beautiful of Face," "Goddess of Charm," and "The Sweetest in Love." To show his great love for her, Ramesses built a temple for Nefertari next to his Great Temple at Abu Simbel. . . . One inscription on the temple reads: "Ramesses built a temple dug in the rock so that it may remain eternally for Queen Nefertari . . . for whom the sun rises."[2]

Iset-Nofret. Her origins are even more obscure than Nefertari's. But some modern scholars think that she was born in Palestine. If so, she would have dropped her foreign birth name and adopted the Egyptian name of Iset-Nofret on joining the king's harem.

Iset-Nofret bore Ramesses at least four children. One was his second son (and second-in-line for the throne after Amunhirwenemef) named Ramesses. She also produced two other sons: Khaemwaset, who became a famous scholar, and Merenptah, who ended up succeeding his father as pharaoh. The fourth child of Ramesses and Iset-Nofret was a daughter, Bintanath.

Bintanath, who was born several years before her mother became queen, was destined to play an important part in Ramesses' life. In the thirty-fourth year of his reign, only a decade after Nefertari's death, Iset-Nofret died, too. Bintanath now became the chief wife and queen. Subsequently, Ramesses turned three more of his daughters into favored consorts— Meritamun (daughter of Nefertari), Nebettawi, and Hentmire. (Hentmire is a shadowy figure who may instead have been the king's sister or niece).

Certainly the marriage of a father to his daughter is taboo and criminal in the modern world. Actually, such marriages were uncommon in ancient Egypt as well. For many centuries, however, the royal family was viewed as an exception. Tradition and propaganda linked the royals to the gods. And religious lore included stories about some male gods mating with their sisters or daughters. The best known example was the relationship between Osiris, lord of the Underworld, and his sister, the fertility goddess Isis. In imitation of these and other gods, a number of pharaohs married their daughters or sisters. Another reason for these rulers to marry their daughters was to keep political power within the family. And the resulting unions were widely accepted both socially and morally throughout Egypt.

 # THE PHARAOH'S FOREIGN WIVES

Two other young women became favorite wives of Ramesses late in his life and reign. Both were the daughters of a Hittite king, Hattusilis III. Ramesses long opposed the Hittites and their empire, centered in Asia Minor. But he eventually saw the wisdom of making peace with them. In time, as relations between the two powers improved, a royal intermarriage was proposed.

The negotiations and preparations for the wedding were extensive and time-consuming. They required many exchanges of letters (carved on small wooden or stone tablets). Each letter had to be carried by a rider who took several weeks to cover the roughly eight hundred miles that separated the two lands. Ramesses was very eager to meet his new bride. This fact is partly revealed by the joyous tone of his response to a letter from the Hittite queen, Pudukhepa, confirming the final details. The letter affords a rare glimpse into Ramesses' private life, thoughts, and emotions.

I have seen the tablet my Sister sent me. [By "my Sister" he means Pudukhepa. "Sister" and "Brother" were commonly used as terms of courtesy among royal heads of state.] And I have noted all the matters on which the

Great Queen of Hatti, my Sister, has so very, very graciously written to me. . . . The Great King, the King of Hatti, my Brother, has written to me, saying, "Let people come, to pour fine oil on my daughter's head [an act symbolizing the sealing of the deal], and may she be brought into the house of the Great King, the King of Egypt!". . . Excellent, excellent is this decision about which my Brother has written to me. Our two great countries will become as one land forever!³

After a long journey, the young woman chosen to be Ramesses' newest bride arrived in Pi-Ramesse, a city he had erected in the eastern Nile Delta. Her Hittite name is not known. This is not surprising considering that she immediately adopted an Egyptian name—Maathorneferure. It meant "The One Who Sees Horus, the Visible Splendor [or beauty] of Ra." (Here, to "see Horus" referred to her getting to know Ramesses. Egyptian pharaohs were thought to be human versions of that god's spirit.)

Maathorneferure bore Ramesses one child—a daughter. This no doubt disappointed Hattusilis, her father, who hoped she would produce a son who might end up succeeding Ramesses on Egypt's throne. The Hittite king also wanted his daughter to receive the status of chief royal wife to Ramesses. But, Ramesses already had a principal wife. Some evidence suggests that the two monarchs negotiated this matter. Maathorneferure was allowed to share the position of chief wife, the only known instance of this happening in ancient Egypt.

In spite of all this fuss about wifely status, however, soon afterwards Maathorneferure faded into obscurity in the official records. Most modern scholars assume she died young. In spite of the tragedy, relations between the two nations remained friendly. A few years later Hattusilis and Pudukhepa sent a second daughter to marry Ramesses. Neither her Hittite name nor her Egyptian name has survived and nothing concrete is known about her.

 THE CHILDREN AND THE SUCCESSION

Just as important to Ramesses as his many wives were his even more numerous children. In fact, for this pharaoh children represented more than just the warmth of family and the joys of parenthood. He was also strongly concerned about his ability to father children. It was thought that the gods could ensure the yearly fertility and renewal of crops and other plants. This was most evident in the yearly flooding of the Nile, which watered the fields and laid down a fresh layer of rich soil. In this way, the gods made Egypt fertile and spared the people from suffering from drought and starvation. In a similar manner, as a living god, or at least a representative of the gods, Egypt's pharaoh was expected to be fertile himself. Ramesses "wanted everyone to be aware of his impressive fertility," Joyce Tyldesly writes,

> a fertility that he saw as an important aspect of his role
> as pharaoh and which was linked at a very basic level to
> the fertility and survival of Egypt and the Nile. And so
> we see his sons and daughters, named and divided by sex,
> [marching] in two single files [in the reliefs carved] along
> the walls of his temples in Egypt and Nubia, where they

AN ARMY OF ROYAL OFFSPRING?

In the late nineteenth century and early twentieth century several scholars made what are now seen as gross overestimates of the numbers of Ramesses' children, grandchildren, and other descendants. Perhaps the most outrageous of these was by Terence Gray in a work titled *And in the Tomb were Found, Or Plays and Portraits of Old Egypt.*

> How literally such a man may have been the "Father of His People" can best be realized by considering [the] large number of children [that Ramesses had] and his long life. For taking them at 400, 200 males and 200 females, allowing for the males 20 children each, and for the females 5, we get 4,000 and 1,000, in all 5,000 grandchildren. Allowing for these 2,500 males and 2,500 females, 10 children each for the males and 2 for the females of this second . . . generation, we get 25,000 and 5,000, in all 30,000 great grandchildren. . . . Moreover, in the lifetime of a century there might well yet be another generation in being, so that, added together, there would be nothing outrageous in Ramesses having up to or well over thirty-five thousand descendants of himself living in Egypt.[4]

Of course, now we know that in reality Ramesses had about one hundred children, and many of these children probably died at a very young age—before they even had children of their own.

represent the living truth of Ramesses' supreme fitness to rule.[5]

Just how fertile was Ramesses? Early modern scholars estimated the number of his children to be as low as 170 and as high as 400. More recent scholarship holds that these numbers are too high. The latest estimates suggest that he had about 45 sons and from 45 to 55 daughters. That makes a total of roughly 90 to 100 offspring. It must be kept in mind that the total number of his living children was lower than this at any given time. This was because infant mortality rates in ancient times were very high. (Infant mortality is the death of babies and young children.) It is probable that as many as 20 or 30 or more of Ramesses' children died before they were five. Others likely died in early adulthood of disease or accidents and did not outlive their father, who survived into extreme old age.

In fact, the survival of certain chosen children was very important to Ramesses. After all, he wanted to ensure a suitable heir to his throne. Moreover, he thought it best to have a few backup candidates in case his first choice did not live long enough to assume power. As the pharaoh's luck would have it, this strategy proved wise. The first in line for the throne, Nefertari's son Amunhirwenemef (renamed Amunhirkhepeshef when Ramesses took the throne), died in his twenties or thirties. The circumstances are unknown. But he was a soldier, so he may have been killed in battle. The second in line, Iset-Nofret's son Ramesses, died, too. That left Nefertari's second son, Prehirwenemef, next in line for

RAMESSES' SON THE FIRST ARCHAEOLOGIST?

Merenptah, who succeeded Ramesses as pharaoh, was not the only one of Ramesses' sons to achieve longlasting fame. In fact, one of Iset-Nofret's sons, Khaemwaset, was more widely remembered than Merenptah in later ancient times.

In his own lifetime Khaemwaset served as high priest of the god Ptah and governor of the city of Memphis. Whatever he did, said, or wrote (little of which has survived) earned him a reputation in later generations as a powerful magician.

More interesting from a modern viewpoint was that Khaemwaset may have been the world's first archaeologist. He took a keen interest in his country's past. And it appears that he discovered and preserved statues and other artifacts from prior centuries. He also inscribed the names of the pharaohs who built many of the country's pyramids on the sides of these monuments.

the throne. But he, like Amunhirkhepeshef, probably died in battle.

After passing over several other sons that he saw as unfit to rule, Ramesses settled on his thirteenth son—Merenptah—another of Iset-Nofret's offspring. Very little is known about Merenptah as a child and even as a young adult. This is because he was already in his sixties when he succeeded his elderly father. Throughout most of his life, therefore, Merenptah was overshadowed by the towering figure of Ramesses. Indeed, for some seven decades Ramesses II proved himself to be as formidable a husband and father as he was an administrator and warrior.

EARLY MILITARY EXPLOITS

In addition to being the chief administrator of Egypt, the pharaoh was the commander-in-chief of the country's armies. He had the authority to declare war or make peace. He decided the overall strategy of a war. And in most cases he led the troops on military campaigns. The pharaoh had to deal with any and all threats to the nation's borders or its larger sphere of influence in the Near East. Thus, when he assumed the throne in about 1279 B.C., Ramesses inherited the huge responsibilities of keeping the country safe and maintaining its empire.

For the most part, that empire did not consist of extensive foreign territories that Egypt ruled directly. Rather, the Egyptians held strong political and economic influence over three neighboring regions. One was Libya, to the west of Egypt. The second was Nubia in the

SYRIA—A VALUABLE ECONOMIC PRIZE

In this except from his book about Ramesses II, military historian Mark Healy explains why the region of Syria was so coveted and fought over by large nation-states such as Egypt and Hatti.

> During this period, Syria was the crossroads of world commerce. Goods from the Aegean [Sea, bordering Greece's eastern coast] and beyond entered the Near East via [Syrian] ports such as Ugarit . . . Underwater excavations of late Bronze Age ships . . . show the remarkable range of goods they carried—copper, tin, chemicals, tools, glass ingots, ivory . . . jewelry, luxury goods, timber, textiles, and foodstuffs. This merchandise was then distributed throughout the Near East and beyond by a network of extensive trade routes. From the east and south, these same land routes were used by merchants who brought raw materials such as precious metals . . . and other merchandise from as far afield as Iran and Afghanistan to trade in the [markets] of Syria. With its inherent fertility and richness in natural resources, Syria therefore offered much to predatory powers seeking to use such wealth for their own benefit. Thirty-three centuries ago, "world" power was synonymous with the control of Syria.[1]

south. Finally there was Syria-Palestine in the east, the large area stretching from the Sinai Peninsula in the south to southern Asia Minor in the north.

As long as the local leaders of the cities and towns of Syria-Palestine were on friendly terms with Egypt, the pharaohs were content. Here, "friendly terms" meant pledging allegiance to Egypt and largely doing its bidding in political matters and trade. If a local ruler or people did not do a pharaoh's bidding, the Egyptians viewed it as a rebellion. The "rebels" were then subject to punishment, including military force.

However, sometimes force was not necessary. In fact, the pharaohs' long-range strategy often involved direct grooming of local foreign rulers to make them think and act like allies. Such grooming usually took place within Egypt itself. It involved learning the Egyptian language and about Egyptian culture. This policy of creating vassal rulers (those expected to do the bidding of Egyptian leaders) was applied particularly in Syria-Palestine during the New Kingdom. In addition, the Egyptians maintained forts manned by soldiers in Syria-Palestine. These soldiers were ordered to keep a watchful eye on the vassal rulers and deal with minor troubles in the region. Egyptologist Ian Shaw, an authority on ancient Egyptian warfare, tells about both of these strategies. He begins with Ramesses' illustrious predecessor, Thutmose III, who had reigned two centuries before:

> Thutmose III backed up his military achievements in Syria-Palestine with the creation of a network of

This needle-shaped monument, called an obelisk, in Istanbul, Turkey, honors the pharaoh Thutmose III. It was moved to Constantinople, Turkey (today Istanbul), by Roman Emperor Theodosius I in 390 B.C. Thutmose ruled two hundred years before Ramesses II.

garrisons and numerous vassal treaties. In his sixth campaign he adopted a more long-term strategy, taking back 36 chiefs' sons to the Egyptian court so that they could be held as hostages, indoctrinated with [taught] Egyptian ideas, and eventually restored to their thrones as puppet rulers. . . . [Meanwhile] at a local level the Egyptian garrisons [forts] in Syria-Palestine were able to police both the vassal cities and the troublesome bands of nomadic peoples [who sometimes moved through the region].[2]

SETI'S EXPEDITION TO KADESH

Once in power, Ramesses aimed to continue this policy of maintaining vassal rulers in Syria–Palestine and teaching their children Egyptian ways. However, he was well aware that this approach did not always produce the desired results. In particular, he remembered what had happened during the reign of his father, Seti. Some of the towns in southern Syria, including Kadesh, had switched their allegiance to the Hittite king. And Seti had felt compelled to lead troops into the region.

The details of Seti's expedition to Kadesh are unclear. As near as modern scholars can tell, he did fight at least one battle against the Hittites. Carved reliefs show that he captured a number of Hittites. And he may have taken control of some of the territory around the town, if only temporarily. According to Seti himself, he accomplished much more:

> Victorious king, who protects Egypt, who cleaves [cuts or drives his way] through the masses of rebellious foreign

lands. He causes the chiefs of [Syria-Palestine] to cease all boasting with their mouths. His strong arm is powerful . . . like [that of a god]. The strong-armed [pharaoh] who overthrows his opponents, who strikes the chiefs of all the foreign lands.[3]

The problem is that this statement does not square with the facts of the situation that existed in the years following the campaign. Seti had not marched any farther north than Kadesh. So he had not "overthrown" the Hittites' homeland (located hundreds of miles away in Asia Minor). Nor had he captured the countries bordering Syria. Shortly after the campaign, Kadesh was once more in Hittite hands. Surviving evidence suggests that Seti's efforts there had achieved little more than a stalemate or temporary truce. Thus, his victory reliefs and inscriptions were likely part of a propaganda campaign he launched when he returned to Egypt. Long before Seti's time, the pharaohs had learned that it was wise not to admit any degree of failure to the people.

More important, Ramesses, then still coregent, had accompanied his father on the Syrian campaign. So later, when he ascended the Egyptian throne, Ramesses was well aware that Kadesh had not been properly secured. He knew that the Hittite presence in that region still posed a serious foreign policy and military problem for Egypt. Moreover, he must have sensed that Seti's expedition had been only a prelude to his own impending adventures in Syria. As Tyldesley puts it, "To Ramesses, Kadesh was unfinished business" and he began "to prepare his soldiers for further action."[4]

The Pharaoh's Army

These soldiers who served Ramesses made up one of the world's earliest large-scale armies. Scholars know very little about the recruitment, training, pay, and daily lives of these troops. But various inscriptions and other ancient sources give a basic idea of the approximate size of the units that made up the New Kingdom army. The largest single unit was a division of five thousand men. Not long before Ramesses' time, probably in the reign of Horemheb, it became standard for the government to maintain four such divisions. They were assigned the names of prominent gods—Amun, Ra, Ptah, and Seth. These four deities were chosen because they had special religious significance for the royal families of the Nineteenth Dynasty.

Although they were part of the larger army, each of the four divisions was a self-contained unit that could operate on its own. So the pharaoh had options that gave him considerable flexibility as commander-in-chief. He could combine the four divisions into one large army for a specific campaign or battle. Or he could give the four groups separate goals and tasks. In fact, they appear to have operated separately much more often than they did as a combined army. For example, as a matter of security, the four divisions did not customarily march through enemy territory together. Instead, they kept apart from one another by a distance of about six miles. They communicated via messengers on horseback. That way, if the enemy ambushed one division, the rest of the army remained intact and ready to strike back.

Each of Ramesses' army divisions had its own commander—a general. The pharaoh appointed these leaders and they reported directly to him. Each maintained his own military base, recruited new soldiers for his division, trained them, disciplined them, and led them on the march. To make organizing, training, and disciplining the troops easier, the generals broke the divisions down into smaller units. As determined by Ian Shaw and other modern experts, a host had 500 men. It was one-tenth of a division. Each host was divided into two companies, both with 250 men. Smaller units included the platoon, with fifty men, and the squad, with ten men. Each host, company, platoon, and squad had its own subleader, who reported to the division general. And aiding all of these officers were several army scribes, highly literate men who kept careful records of the troops and supplies. (These records, some of which have survived, were recorded on papyrus, a kind of paper made from a water plant that grew in abundance in the Nile Valley.)

LARGE SUPPLIES OF LETHAL WEAPONS

Ramesses counted on the army divisions, officers, and troops to make his expedition into Syria-Palestine a success. But experience had taught him that simply having a big, well-organized army was not enough. The soldiers had to have effective, lethal weapons and be trained in their use. In this regard, Ramesses had an advantage over most of his enemies. Making new weapons in quantity and teaching large numbers of troops to use them were huge, very expensive endeavors. Only the largest, most populous, and richest countries could afford to arm tens of thousands of troops with top-notch weapons. This was a major reason why Egypt was so often able to strong-arm smaller, less populous states into submission.

Some of these weapons wielded by Ramesses' troops were standard ones for that time. Egyptian troops (as well as enemy soldiers) had been using them for many centuries. One was the battle-ax, for slicing through enemy armor and helmets. Originally it had featured a sharpened stone blade. But by the New Kingdom more durable bronze blades were the norm. Ramesses' foot soldiers also carried spears (for jabbing) and javelins (throwing spears).

In addition, large numbers of Egyptian troops were armed with the *khopesh*, a sword originally introduced into Egypt from Palestine. The khopesh had a curved blade similar to that of the sickles that the farmers of that time used to cut wheat. (The difference was that the sword blade was a good deal smaller than a sickle blade.) The key to the effective use of the khopesh was its finely sharpened outer edge. A soldier swung the sword outward in a slashing movement. A sideways stroke could slice open an opponent's throat or sever a hamstring. And an up-and-down stroke could cut off a hand or ear.

The battle-ax, spear, javelin, and khopesh were all designed for close-in fighting, at or near the enemy's ranks. The Egyptians also had a very effective long-range weapon—the composite bow. Introduced into Egypt at the dawn of the New Kingdom, this weapon had originated in Mesopotamia (what is now Iraq). An ordinary bow (known as a simple bow) was made from a single piece of wood. In contrast, a composite bow combined a number of different materials. These included animal horns and tendons as well as wood. The result was a weapon of far greater power than the traditional bow. With the composite version, troops could spray enemy ranks with arrows from a distance of up to a third of a mile.

THE CENTERPIECE OF RAMESSES' ARMY

Some Egyptian foot soldiers likely carried composite bows. But this weapon was especially effective and lethal in the hands of warriors mounted on chariots. Indeed, surviving paintings and sculptures indicate that Ramesses' chariot corps was the centerpiece of his army. Like the composite bow, the battle chariot had made its way to Egypt from Mesopotamia. And it became a standard weapon in the early New Kingdom. Compared to swords, axes, bows, and other handheld weapons, chariots were very expensive to build and maintain. It took skilled woodworkers to construct these vehicles. Also, large tracts of land were needed to pasture the horses that pulled them. Thus, only the richest countries, such as Egypt and Hatti, could afford to own large-scale chariot divisions and to take them along on military campaigns.

STRUCTURE OF A WAR CHARIOT

Egyptian chariots of the New Kingdom era were very lightweight yet sturdy. A typical chariot had three principal parts. The first was the body of the vehicle, consisting of a wooden frame with a base about a meter [3.3 feet] wide and half a meter long. The height of the front rim of the chariot was 75 centimeters [29 inches]. So the front section covered the charioteer to a point about half way up his thighs. Most sections of the chariot's platform and sides were covered by leather. The second principal part of the chariot consisted of the axle and wheels. The axle itself was about 6 centimeters [2.4 inches] thick at the center and stretched roughly 1.23 meters [4.1 feet] from wheel to wheel. Each wheel had four spokes. Finally came the chariot's pole, which ran under the body of the vehicle and attached to the yoke by nails. The horses that pulled the chariot were connected to the yoke. The entire construction of the vehicle was designed for lightness, speed, and maneuverability.

As for the construction of Egyptian chariots, they were made of lightweight wood. So the horses harnessed to them had less weight to pull and could run faster. Lighter chariots were also more maneuverable. Indeed, the ability to turn the vehicle sharply and quickly was essential to its success on the battlefield. Also essential was a skilled driver. He coordinated the chariot's charges and other movements with a warrior who stood directly behind him on the moving platform. The warrior first fired arrows at the enemy from a distance. Then, after the chariot made contact with the enemy lines, the warrior hurled javelins, a supply of which he carried on board.

One disadvantage of Ramesses' chariots was that they could not be used for shock tactics (crashing into and mowing down enemy soldiers). These vehicles gave up a certain amount of solidity and strength so that they could be faster and more maneuverable. Thus, they were much too fragile for shock charges. In contrast, Hittite chariots were heavier and *could* be used for shock tactics.

 ## THREATS CLOSE TO HOME

Whatever the enemy's strengths and capabilities, Ramesses' overall goal seems never to have been in doubt. He was eager to dislodge the Hittites and their influence from Syria. So from the very beginning of his reign, he began preparing for a campaign into that border region.

However, though itching for a fight with the Hittites, Ramesses was not foolhardy. First, he appreciated the importance of taking the time to make proper and careful preparations for such a large-scale expedition. Also, for the time being his attention was diverted by more pressing threats closer to home.

The first of these threats came from the sea. No sooner had Ramesses ascended the throne when messengers brought him word of trouble in the Nile Delta region. Pirates had been raiding ships and attacking villages located near the coast. Ramesses immediately dealt with the pirates. He learned that they were members of a people known as the Sherden, who hailed from northern Syria or southern Asia Minor. Although they were good fighters, he had no trouble subduing them. The new pharaoh then displayed wisdom as well as strength by recruiting the captured Sherden into his army rather than killing them.

Another threat took the form of nomadic tribes from Libya. In the final years of Seti's reign, groups of Libyans had begun moving into the western Delta. Ramesses decided that the best way to deal with the problem was to build forts along Egypt's desert frontier with Libya. The total number of forts he built is unknown. But the remains of five have been discovered to date and there may well have been as many as fifteen or more. Built of mud-bricks, the walls of some of these installations were as high as forty feet. They were also wisely constructed around key oases (areas of land with a water source and trees) in the desert. That way Ramesses controlled the region's water supplies, which were essential to any nomads trying to cross the desert to Egypt.

RAMESSES' FIRST SYRIAN CAMPAIGN

Having secured the country's sea coast and western desert, Ramesses finally turned his full attention to the eastern frontier and Syria-Palestine. In the summer of his fourth year as pharaoh (ca. 1275 B.C.), he led his army across the Sinai Peninsula and into Palestine. It appears that the area of Canaan (future site of the Kingdom of Israel) was still loyal to Egypt. The same was true of Byblos, Tyre, and other coastal cities inhabited by Phoenicians. (The Phoenicians were a seafaring people known for their fine ships and widespread trade relations). Thus, no military action was required until the Egyptians reached southern Syria.

The Syrian city-state of Amurru, not far from Kadesh, *had* gone over to the Hittites. However, Ramesses encountered no Hittite forces in the area. So he must have had little trouble in retaking Amurru. The exact way he managed this is unknown. He did set up stelae in the area bearing inscriptions describing his exploits. But as the late scholar James H. Breasted pointed out, "these stelae are so weathered that the records of the campaign which they doubtless contained are almost totally illegible [unreadable]."[5]

Also unclear is why Ramesses returned to Egypt without pressing on to Kadesh or perhaps even further into Hittite territory. It could well be that he did not want to overextend his army's long supply lines. These required the services of many people and were extremely expensive and difficult to maintain. Military historian Mark Healy explains:

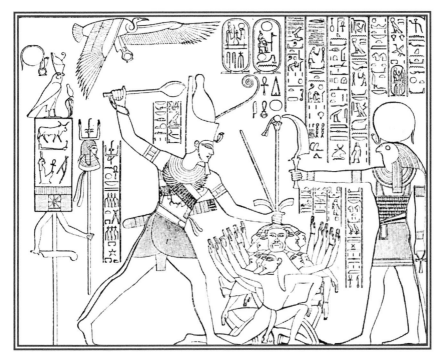

In this illustration, Ramesses kills soldiers from nearby enemy nations. To his right stands the god Horus, who was sometimes known as "the slaughterer."

> Although the Egyptian army possessed a well-organized [food-supply system], the feeding of a large . . . force on the move through Canaan and northwards to Syria was heavily dependent on the provision of supplies provided by vassal [subservient] rulers along the line of march. . . . Once away from the territories under firm Egyptian control, the army would need to fall back upon stored provisions carried in wagons drawn by oxen. . . . Notwithstanding the undoubted efficiency of the scribes who oversaw the provision of supplies . . . Bronze Age [supply operations] were simply not up to the task of catering to the needs of all the troops in an [army] on the march. . . . [Most of the soldiers] were forced . . . to live off the land.[6]

Thus, Ramesses likely felt that his most cost-effective option was to return home. There, he could regroup and replenish his supplies. Then he could return to Syria the following year and finish the job he had started there.

 ## "LET US FIGHT!"

Probably long before the army made it back to Egypt, the Hittite king, Muwatallis II, received word of Ramesses' arrival in Syria. Hatti's ruler was clearly angry over what he saw as Egyptian meddling in his affairs. Words to that effect must have appeared in a war declaration delivered to Ramesses by a Hittite messenger. The text has not survived but was undoubtedly similar to an earlier Hittite war declaration that *has* survived. It reads in part: "My subjects who went over to you, when I demanded them

THE ESSENTIAL DUTIES OF ARMY SCRIBES

In addition to a general and his staff of officers, each Egyptian army division had several army scribes. They reported not only to the general who commanded their division, but also to a higher-ranking scribe who oversaw all the scribes in the pharaoh's army. That highest-ranking scribe then reported directly to the pharaoh or to his vizier (chief civilian administrator).

The army scribes had a number of important duties that were essential to keeping the army bases and campaign operations running smoothly. First, the scribes maintained up-to-date lists of all new recruits, retired soldiers, and dead and wounded troops. Another duty of army scribes was to order, organize, and keep track of stocks of food, weapons, and other supplies. Still another essential scribal duty was to decide what jobs needed to be done in camp or on the march and to assign workers to do those jobs. Clearly, without its staff of skilled, hard-working scribes, the Egyptian army could not function on a daily basis.

back from you, you did not restore them to me. . . . Up then! Let us fight, and let the Storm-god, my lord, decide our case!"[7]

Muwatallis wasted no time in making good on his threat to fight the Egyptians. Egyptian sources claim that he assembled some thirty-seven thousand foot soldiers and twenty-five hundred chariots and marched south toward Syria.

Ramesses now faced a very different situation than he had in his first foray into that region. This time a huge enemy force would be waiting for him. But he had no intention of backing down from the challenge. In the spring of the fifth year of his reign, he once more assembled the divisions of Amun, Ra, Ptah, and Seth and marched them into Palestine.

The first stop in the journey north was in the coastal area now known as Gaza. For reasons that are now unclear, Ramesses divided his forces in an unusual way. He drew men from one or more of his four main divisions. These soldiers formed a fifth division. Ancient sources call them *Ne'arin*, which translates as "young men" or "recruits." Modern scholars are unsure why Ramesses did this and have speculated a great deal about who these troops were. One theory holds that they were elite Palestinian soldiers who fought within the Egyptian army.

Whatever the identity of these troops may have been, Ramesses told them to march along the coast.

He ordered them to make sure the towns there were loyal and then meet him later at Kadesh. He and the main army continued north through the Bekka Valley, the usual inland route taken by Egyptian armies in the region. The Bekka Valley lies many miles inland from the sea. This means that the *Ne'arin* were for a while completely cut off from the main body of the pharaoh's army. And they would not be able to help if the main units got into a fight on their way to Kadesh.

It appears that this was a risk that Ramesses was willing to take. As the main body of the army moved northward through the Bekka Valley, he personally led the Amun division, which marched out ahead of the others. No letters or other documents have survived to reveal what was going through his mind. But a man of Ramesses' intelligence and experience had to realize one thing. At the very least, he was heading toward a great date with destiny.

5

RIVER OF BLOOD

As Ramesses led the Amun division across the Orontes River and onto the plain of Kadesh, he had no idea that he and his troops were walking into a deadly trap. The day before, two local men had told the pharaoh he had nothing to fear. The Hittite king, Muwatallis, was afraid to face Ramesses, they said; Muwatallis had camped his army far to the north. Ramesses had accepted this story. He did not realize that the men who told it were agents of Muwatallis, who had ordered them to lie. The Hittite king and his large army were in fact hidden on the other side of Kadesh.

Only after the Egyptians had made camp in front of the city did Ramesses learn the truth. Under torture, some captured Hittite spies admitted that Muwatallis was actually nearby and ready to ambush the Egyptians. It was now clear to Ramesses that a major battle was about to take place.

The pharaoh had to be deeply worried for two reasons. First, his camp was pitched in the open plain, where he and his men were open to a sudden attack on all sides. Second, the other units of Ramesses' army did not yet know that the enemy was lurking nearby. They had to be warned, if there was indeed still time enough to warn them.

These were the basic realities of the scene near Kadesh on that April day in 1274 B.C. One huge army lay hidden, its soldiers in full battle gear and ready to fight. Nearby, another large army lay divided and almost completely unprepared to fight. The stage was set for one of the largest and most important battles in the long history of the Near East.

The Battle of Kadesh turned out to be of great importance to later scholars as well. This is because it is the only battle of the Old, Middle, and New Kingdoms for which a specific event-by-event account can be reconstructed. It is also the first battle in world history for which a detailed account exists. This account takes the form of a series of carved reliefs, accompanied by inscribed texts, commissioned after the war by Ramesses. At least fifteen separate copies of the battle story were created on the walls of temples at Abydos, Karnak, Abu Simbel, and elsewhere. They remain the chief sources of Ramesses' reputation as one of Egypt's great warrior kings. (No Hittite descriptions of the battle have survived.)

 # THE HITTITES AMBUSH RA

At the time, of course, Ramesses was not thinking about reliefs, inscriptions, or what people in the far future would think about him. His attention was fixed on the dire dilemma he and his men found themselves in at that moment. The pharaoh considered the possibility that the enemy army might suddenly swarm around Kadesh and engulf the Egyptian camp.

Ramesses was also worried about the other units of his army, especially the Ra division. It had just crossed the Orontes, a few miles south of Ramesses' camp. The men of Ra were strung out in long lines on the open plain, easy targets for a Hittite ambush. Moreover, the Ptah and Seth divisions would surely walk into the same trap in a matter of a few hours. Acting quickly, the pharaoh summoned his best horsemen and told them to ride at top speed to warn the other divisions of the impending danger.

But it was too late. Only a few minutes after the horsemen galloped out of Ramesses' camp, the jaws of the Hittite trap began to snap shut on the troops of Ra. As they marched along, a large number of Muwatallis' chariots appeared seemingly out of nowhere. The Hittites charged directly into the Egyptians, who were unprepared for battle. Ra's ranks swiftly fell into disorder as the Hittite chariots smashed their way through them.

In this first contact between the enemy armies, the differences in size and fighting tactics of the opposing chariots immediately became apparent. The Hittite vehicles were wide and heavy, while the Egyptian chariots were slender and lightweight. Indeed, the Hittite chariots looked more like miniature wagons, with stout wooden planks making up the floors and sides. Also, unlike the two-man crew of an Egyptian chariot, a

Hittite chariot carried a crew of three. In addition to the driver and warrior, there was a shield-bearer who protected the other two men.

Still another difference in the two fighting systems was the nature of the weaponry and the tactics connected with them. The Hittite chariot warrior used a long thrusting spear. With this weapon he stabbed enemy foot soldiers as his vehicle sped through their ranks. Thus, the Hittite chariots were effectively designed for shock tactics. The combination of their weight and close-in fighting methods allowed them easily to slice through and heavily damage Ra's ranks.

This is all that remains of the King's Gate, part of the city of Hattusas, built about 1650 B.C., in the Hittite Old Kingdom.

RAMESSES' CAMP IS SURROUNDED

In the chaos, the surviving men of the Ra division panicked and began to run. As they headed northward, toward the Egyptian camp, they and the pursuing Hittite chariots kicked up a cloud of dust visible over a great distance. Some of the troops in Ramesses' camp saw this dust and assumed it was a sign of the approaching enemy. They spread the alarm and Ramesses ordered his troops to prepare for battle. Soon his worst fears were confirmed as the frightened and exhausted men of Ra began entering the camp. The pharaoh now realized that almost a quarter of his army had been knocked out of action by the enemy. Worse, that enemy would strike his camp within minutes.

Ramesses hurried to prepare himself for battle. According to his official account:

> When his majesty caught sight of them [the approaching Hittites], he rose quickly, enraged at them, like his father Montu [the Egyptian war god]. . . . Taking up weapons and donning his armor, he was like [the formidable god] Seth in the moment of his power.
>
> He mounted his [chariot, pulled by his prized horses named] "Victory in Thebes" [and "Mut is Content"], and started out quickly alone by himself. His majesty was mighty, his heart stout, [and] one could not stand before him.[1]

This section of the account is believable. It probably fairly accurately depicts the pharaoh's personal preparations for the fight. (However, the part about him riding out all alone is probably exaggerated. Most likely he had bodyguards.)

In contrast, the next portion of the account lapses into gross exaggeration and pure fable. Clearly it was propaganda intended to make the people back home think that Ramesses was a one-man army:

> All his ground [i.e., the ground under him] was ablaze with fire. He burned all the countries with his blast [of fury]. His eyes were savage as he beheld them [the Hittites]. His power flared like fire against them. . . . His Majesty charged into the forces of the foe from Hatti. . . . His majesty slew the entire forces of the foe from Hatti, together with his great chiefs and all his brothers . . . [and] their infantry and their chariotry, falling on their faces one upon the other. His Majesty slaughtered them.[2]

As in nearly all official Egyptian battle accounts, the artists and scribes were careful to avoid any mention of the pharaoh's moments of weakness. Instead, the custom was to stress his strengths and exaggerate his personal role in any victorious moments or events. It was not merely a matter of inflating the pharaoh's ego, however. Like other pharaohs before him, he was believed to be a god by the Egyptian people. So the official accounts of such military events took on a sort of mythological, larger-than-life air.

In an effort to piece together what really happened, modern scholars have learned to read between the lines of the official account. They give Ramesses credit for bravery in the face of extreme danger. But they find it more credible that his initial role in the battle consisted of rallying his soldiers. It is more likely, they say, that he spent much of the time urging them to be firm and hold their ground.

For example, a later section of the official account contains a striking and revealing incident. It took place after the Egyptian camp had been surrounded and the battle was in full swing. The pharaoh, who describes the incident himself, urges one of his followers to shake off his fear and face the enemy. The account mentions the man by name and quotes his verbal exchange with the pharaoh. So it is probably based on a real incident. Ramesses recalled:

> Now, when Menena, my shield-bearer, saw that a large number of [enemy] chariots surrounded [us], he became weak and faint-hearted, great fear invading his body. He said to [me], "My good lord . . . we stand alone in the midst of battle. . . . [Why] do you stand [your ground and continue to fight]? Let us get clear and save [ourselves], Ramesses!" [I] said to the shield-bearer, "Stand firm [and] steady your heart! . . . Why do you fear these weaklings?"[3]

THE TIDE OF BATTLE TURNS

In reconstructing this portion of the battle, therefore, it is safe to assume that the pharaoh rode back and forth among his trapped men. As he did so, he urged them to be brave and fight hard. Scholars point out that such a situation was not unique in the ancient world. Centuries later, the renowned Roman general Julius Caesar and his men were on an expedition in Gaul (now France and Belgium). They suddenly found themselves trapped in their army camp by a much larger force of well-armed attackers. Caesar fearlessly ran back and forth through the camp, rallying his soldiers. He also personally fought enemy warriors who had managed to get inside the camp. His courageous leadership inspired his men to fight with renewed passion. And they succeeded in driving the enemy back and winning the battle.

Most modern historians think that Ramesses performed in a similar manner at Kadesh. A talented and quick-thinking commander, he saw that the Egyptian situation was far from hopeless. True, he and his men were surrounded. Yet much of the force of the Hittite chariot charge had been broken by the physical elements of the camp itself. "As the [Hittite] warriors washed over the mass of Egyptian troops at the western end of the camp," Mark Healy suggests,

> their surge was already beginning to dissipate [weaken]. Chariots slowed as the numerous tents, stores [of supplies], and other impediments became as rocks breaking the tide [of the charge]. Amid the chaos of panicking Egyptian soldiers, those [sentries] who had been [guarding the camp] throughout the night sensed the slowing of the Hittite drive and advanced with *khopesh* and spear in hand to attack the enemy. A desperate hand-to-hand [fight] ensued as the Egyptians pulled down Hittite crews from their [chariots]. . . . Chariots slowed to a crawl as horses struggled vainly to move forward.[4]

As more and more Hittite chariots arrived on the scene, they bunched up behind the ones halted in the camp. This created the equivalent of a modern traffic jam. Ramesses shrewdly took advantage of the situation. Mustering as many of his own chariots as he could, he led them out of the camp and onto the open plain. With all the raised dust and confusion, most of the Hittites did not see this maneuver. The well-trained Egyptian charioteers quickly formed a line. Ramesses took his position in front of the others and at his command the chariots of the Amun division surged forward. Raising their deadly composite bows, the warriors let loose a rain of arrows on the stalled column of enemy chariot crews. Volley after volley of arrows showered the column as the Egyptian chariots swept back and forth before it. (The charioteers carefully kept their distance from the Hittites. They were not trained to make direct charges into the enemy ranks.)

ATTACK AND COUNTERATTACK

So far, the fight could not be called a true chariot battle because the Hittite vehicles were immobile and largely sitting targets. However, that situation rapidly changed. Some of the Hittite charioteers who were further away from the camp saw what was happening to their comrades. So they counterattacked by charging right at the Egyptian chariots.

But by this time the Hittites' horses were exhausted from hours of activity with little rest. So the charge was slow and ponderous. Moreover, the heavy Hittite

THE COMPOSITE BOW

One of the main advantages possessed by Egyptian troops in the battle at Kadesh was the composite bow, which had been introduced into Egypt a little more than two centuries before. The four principal materials in this bow were wood, animal horn, animal tendons (sinew), and glue. The wooden parts often contained three or four kinds of wood, each having a certain desired amount of flexibility. The harder animal horn was used in spots where more rigidity was desired. The bow-maker applied  the sinews to the weapon to increase its springing power. Due to the skillful combination of these diverse materials, the composite bow could fire an arrow up to five or six hundred yards. (Such long shots were not very accurate, however. The best archers could achieve considerable accuracy up to one or two hundred yards.)

vehicles, designed for shock tactics, were not very maneuverable. Yet, the lightweight Egyptian chariots were nimble and swift. Ramesses and his men darted to and fro, avoiding direct contact with the enemy vehicles, which had trouble turning around. Meanwhile, the Egyptians kept up a barrage of arrows, inflicting horrific damage on the Hittite crews. It did not help the Hittites that they did not have their infantry to back them up. Expecting a swift victory, Muwatallis had made the mistake of sending only chariots against Ra and Amun.

Eventually, the remaining Hittite charioteers saw that further fighting would be useless. With their last ounces of energy, they turned and began to flee. Seeing this, Ramesses regrouped his own forces and gave chase. At the same time, the foot soldiers of Amun and Ra entered the fray. They had been watching the chariot battle from the battered camp, and now they dashed forward to join the Egyptian chariots.

It is unclear what Muwatallis was doing during these early stages of the battle. Ramesses' official account makes it sound as if the Hittite king watched the whole event from some nearby vantage. "The wretched Chief of Kheta," the account states, "stood among his troops and chariots, watching His Majesty [Ramesses] fight." The account also claims that Muwatallis showed fear at the sight of the Egyptian army in action: "[He] stood turning, shrinking, afraid."[5] It is much more likely, however, that the Hittite monarch remained in a safe position on the other side of Kadesh. If so, following custom, he received constant reports of the ongoing battle from riders.

Whether or not Muwatallis was afraid, he did have sufficient reason to worry. His chariots had failed to take the Egyptian camp and were now in full retreat. Still, he realized that all was not lost because he had not yet sent in the bulk of his troops. He still had a thousand chariots ready for action. Many of these were manned by Hittite noblemen and the chiefs of Hittite vassal states. Muwatallis also had his tens of thousands of foot soldiers ready to enter the fray. Wasting no time, he ordered a large portion of these forces to cross the Orontes and attack Ramesses' army from the rear.

 ## UNEXPECTED REINFORCEMENTS

Muwatallis had every reason to believe that he now had Ramesses in another trap. The Hittite reserves were launching an assault on the enemy's rear. Meanwhile, the fleeing Hittite chariots might turn on the Egyptians, who would then be caught in the middle. Hittite messengers had already assured Muwatallis that the Ptah and Seth divisions were still too far away to help the Egyptians. Therefore, ultimate victory seemed within the Hittite ruler's grasp.

What Muwatallis's messengers apparently did not tell him—perhaps because they simply did not know—was that Ramesses had a fifth army unit at his disposal. The *Ne'arin*, whom the pharaoh had sent up the Palestinian coast a few weeks earlier, had finished their mission. In fact, they were already nearing Kadesh during the early stages of the battle. Advanced scouts from the *Ne'arin* force saw what was happening and hurried back to their unit. Leaving their infantry behind to catch up when they could, the *Ne'arin* charioteers drove toward Kadesh at top speed. And they arrived just as Muwatallis' reserve forces were crossing the Orontes.

The *Ne'arin* charioteers seized the moment. Placing themselves between Ramesses' units and the Hittites, they formed a battle line and charged across the plain at the surprised enemy. As Healy tells it:

> The *Ne'arin* unleashed massed volleys of arrows into the ranks of the Hittites. Unable to close with their enemy, [these Hittite warriors] could not defend themselves. The Hittite force visibly wavered, then began to retreat, its own passage back to the river made doubly horren-dous by the appearance from the south of Ramesses and elements of his chariotry. . . . In a running battle all the way back to the river, the Egyptians poured a [devastating] fire from their composite bows into the now rapidly depleting Hittite ranks. . . . Desperate to save their lives, the leading [Hittite] charioteers plunged into the Orontes in an [effort] to escape the rapidly closing Egyptians.[6]

Weighed down by their armor, or crushed by their own chariots, many Hittites died. And the river ran red with blood.

 ## A LION AMONG GOATS

By the end of the day, Ramesses, the remaining men of Ra and Amun, and the *Ne'arin* had driven all the surviving Hittites back across the river. King Muwatallis still had many more troops in reserve. In fact, the bulk of his army was still intact. But he felt it unwise to launch any further attacks. For one thing, the Egyptians now held a commanding position on their side of the Orontes. Also, word came that the Ptah and Seth divisions were fast approaching to reinforce Ramesses' ranks.

Consequently, Muwatallis decided to withdraw and return to Hatti. As for Ramesses, some evidence suggests that he wanted to renew the battle the next day. However, his generals convinced him that this would not be a wise move. They may have argued that the surviving Egyptian troops were too exhausted to perform at their peak capacity. Of course, Ramesses' official account of the battle gave a different reason for why the battle did not resume. The account claimed that the Hittite king was afraid and recognized that he had been beaten. Supposedly, before he retreated Muwatallis begged for mercy, saying:

> Do not overwhelm us, son of Ra. Lo, your might is great, your strength is heavy upon the land of Hatti. . . . Be not hard in your dealings, victorious king! Peace is better than fighting. [We beg you to] give us breath![7]

This was more of Ramesses' propaganda, however. In reality, both armies had suffered significant numbers of casualties. Neither could claim a clear-cut victory. Moreover, Muwatallis saw no reason to admit defeat or plead for mercy. He still had plenty of troops left and could easily raise many more back in Hatti. Despite the claims of total victory made in his own propaganda,

RAMESSES CALLS ON AMUN FOR AID

One of the passages in Ramesses' official account of the Battle of Kadesh (as translated in Miraim Lichtheim's *Ancient Egyptian Literature*) claims that at the beginning of the struggle the pharaoh had to fight all by himself. Supposedly, all of his troops were too afraid to join him in the fray. So he called on the god Amun for strength and help and attacked the enemy army on his own. Modern scholars consider this a classic piece of propaganda, designed to inflate Ramesses' image as a superior warrior and a living god. "No officer was with me, no charioteer," the passage begins.

> No soldier of my army, no shield-bearer; my infantry, my chariotry yielded before them [the Hittites]. Not one of them stood firm to fight with them. [I] spoke: "What is this, father Amun? Is it right for a father to ignore his son? Are my deeds a matter for you to ignore? . . . Too great is he, the great lord of Egypt, to allow aliens to step on his path! What are those Asiatics to you, O Amun, the wretches ignorant of god? . . . I call to you, my father Amun. I am among a host of strangers. . . . I am alone; there's none with me! My numerous troops have deserted me." [Amun answered the pharaoh, saying:] "Forward, [for] I am with you, I, your father, my hand is with you. I [am able to] prevail over a hundred thousand men. I am lord of victory, lover of valor!"[8]

Ramesses was aware of this reality. He knew that his dispute with the Hittites was not over.

Yet, the young pharaoh did not hesitate to enjoy the chorus of cheers and thanksgiving that awaited him on his return to Egypt. Ramesses was compared to "a wild lion in a valley of goats." He "who goes forth in valor, returns in triumph," stated an inscription composed to praise him. And it was said that the gods had granted him dominion over all lands. These would lie "prostrate [flattened] under his feet forever and all time."[9] At this moment, it must have seemed to many Egyptians that Ramesses had reached the height of his reign. In their view, no later achievement could possibly top what he had accomplished at Kadesh. Time, however, would prove them wrong.

6

MAKING PEACE

When he returned to Egypt from his Syrian expedition, Ramesses told his people that he had achieved a great victory. He had trampled the wretched Hittites into the dust. The enemy king had begged for a truce and an end to the fighting. All across Egypt, official descriptions of the battle hailed Ramesses as a great hero.

The Egyptian people seem to have believed this version of the events. However, most of the people of Palestine did not. Neither did the Hittite people and their vassals believe the story. Ramesses had failed to capture Kadesh, they pointed out. Instead, he had marched his battered army away. Moreover, in the wake of his retreat the Hittites followed and retook the city of Amurru, which the pharaoh had only recently captured. In fact, people of several of the city-states in Palestine were sure that Ramesses' campaign was a failure. So they began openly defying the Egyptians. Meanwhile, back in Hatti, Muwatallis claimed that he, not Ramesses, had been the overwhelming victor.

Which of these markedly different versions of the events at Kadesh was true? After studying all of the surviving evidence, modern scholars have concluded that the truth lay somewhere between the two extremes of the conflicting accounts. According to Trevor Bryce, a noted authority on the Hittites:

> The likelihood is that, after a desperate rally from Ramesses and the forces immediately at his disposal, the Egyptian army was saved at the eleventh hour from a devastating defeat . . . by a very timely arrival of reinforcements [the *Ne'arin*]. . . . And the battle itself ended in a stalemate. Both sides sustained heavy losses and neither emerged as the decisive victor.[1]

Often, however, the true character of an event and the *perception* of that event can be very different. The perception that Ramesses won the battle was confined strictly to Egypt. To Ramesses' dismay, beyond Egypt's borders the perception was that the Hittites had been victorious and had maintained control of Syria. And it was this latter perception that seems to have shaped his foreign policy in that region in the years that followed. He launched many more campaigns to solidify Egypt's control of Syria-Palestine. These conflicts heavily drained his country's resources and hurt the morale of his people. Considering these difficulties, perhaps the pharaoh eventually came to believe that making peace with the enemy was a far better alternative than endless war that would cost the lives of thousands.

RAMESSES' LATER SYRIAN CAMPAIGNS

As the evidence shows, it took a while for Ramesses to learn the lesson that peace is better than war. Clearly, he was not ready to make peace with the Hittites in the years immediately following the confrontation at Kadesh. In fact, in this period he found himself almost constantly involved in efforts to keep his empire in Syria-Palestine intact.

Trouble erupted in the region right after the pharaoh returned to Egypt in self-proclaimed triumph. Ramesses' messengers told him that several towns in Palestine had rebelled against Egyptian control. He knew that he could not sit back and ignore the situation. Otherwise, he would be forced to admit that the entire Kadesh expedition had achieved nothing. The rebels had to be brought back into the Egyptian fold. Also, the Hittites must not be allowed to extend their influence to Egypt's very borders.

The surviving records of the campaigns Ramesses launched into Palestine in the sixth through eighteenth years of his reign are few and in very bad condition. So it is very difficult to piece together anything more than a general snapshot of these expeditions. Most likely each took place in the spring and/or summer. The pharaoh and his troops returned to Egypt in the early fall.

Ramesses seems to have spent the summer of his sixth regnal year (ca. 1273 B.C.) laying siege to the town of Askalon, in southern Palestine. Some surviving sections of an Egyptian relief at Karnak (near Thebes) show the pharaoh's troops storming the city. In the sculpture, Ramesses stands in his chariot and charges at an enemy battle line that has formed on the plain in front of the city. Meanwhile, Egyptian troops climb scaling ladders placed against the city walls. And an Egyptian officer uses a large ax to chop away at the city's main wooden gate.

Askalon and other southern Palestinian towns eventually fell to Ramesses. Moving farther north, he spent his eighth and ninth regnal years fighting near the Sea of Galilee (now in northern Israel). Then he marched northwestward to assault the cities of Tunip and Dapur. The attack on Dapur is the best-documented episode in these campaigns. Carved reliefs showing Ramesses' siege of the city have survived at his mortuary temple, the Ramesseum, and the great temple at Luxor (near Thebes). Inscriptions accompanying the carvings describe the pharaoh's daring. In one celebrated incident, he seems to have ridden to the battlefield without bothering to don his armor (although he did put it on later):

> His Majesty actually did it twice in the presence of his troops and chariotry, while leading them, attacking this Hittite enemy city which is in the region of the city of Tunip in the land of Naharin [Ne'arin]. His Majesty took up his coat-of-mail [armor] to wear it [only after] he had already spent 2 hours standing and attacking the city of the Hittite foe, in front of his troops and chariotry, [without] a coat-of-mail on him. Only then did His Majesty come back to pick up his coat-of-mail again, to

A Storm that Destroys All Enemies

A finely-made relief sculpture on a wall at Ramesses' mortuary temple, the Ramesseum, shows the pharaoh's assault on the walled Syrian city of Dapur. One of the inscriptions accompanying the relief (as translated by Kenneth Kitchen) reinforces Ramesses' image as an invincible warrior who devastates all who oppose him:

> The good god [i.e. Ramesses], strong in valor in the foreign countries, stout-hearted in the fray [fight], resolute [firm] with the chariot, splendid with the chariot. When he [Ramesses] has grasped the bow, he is one who shoots and captures [the enemy] effectively, and he just cannot miss! . . . He is a storm upon the foreign countries, loud of war cry, who raises cataclysm [disaster, or chaos] against the [enemy] chiefs, to plunder their cities, turning all their places into reddened mounds [of earth].[2]

put it on. Now, he had spent 2 hours attacking the hostile Hittite city . . . without wearing his [armor]![3]

 # Exhaustion for All Involved

The Egyptians conducted similar sieges, along with raids and other skirmishes, off and on in Syria-Palestine for at least another eight years. In each episode, Hittite troops were present. Sometimes they were soldiers in a fort Muwatallis had built to control a city. Other times the Hittite troops had been sent to help the local rebels fight the Egyptians. Either way, these encounters kept tensions between the two great powers—Egypt and Hatti—high. An all-out war between these Near Eastern Superpowers seemed always to linger on the political horizon.

These campaigns resulted in a large amount of death and destruction. Yet all of the surviving evidence suggests that they accomplished little in the long run. Ramesses would succeed in capturing a city. But as soon as he and his troops moved on, its inhabitants would rebel again, forcing the pharaoh to return and fight again. These expeditions were therefore extremely draining for the Egyptians. Each year Ramesses lost more valuable soldiers and supplies. Yet the region never seemed to remain at peace for very long.

Moreover, the yearly conflicts in Syria-Palestine were equally draining and exhausting for the Hittites. In fact, they found themselves in an increasingly dangerous political and military position. In the south they faced losses of men, supplies, and prestige at the hands of the Egyptians. Meanwhile, in the southeast, and much closer to Hatti's borders, a third great Near Eastern power was fast rising. This was the kingdom of Assyria. It was based in the region between the Tigris and Euphrates rivers (in what is now Iraq). At this time, the Assyrians did not pose much of a threat to the Hittite empire and homeland. However, the potential for the continued growth of Assyrian power was very real.

Also, Ramesses saw that this situation played right into his hands. Partly because of the presence of Assyria and its potential for growth, the Hittites were unwilling to commit their full forces to the struggle against him. Perhaps in the future, he reasoned, Assyria might pose a threat to Egypt, too. But for the moment the Assyrian factor worked in his favor. So, he did not try to interfere with Assyria's expansion. (As it turned out, this decision did not bode well for later Egyptian rulers and affairs. Over time the Assyrian Empire did expand in size and power. And in the seventh century B.C., the Assyrians invaded Egypt, causing much death, destruction, and misery.)

RAMESSES CONTROVERSIAL GUEST

Ramesses also benefited from the fallout of a severe political crisis within the borders of Hatti itself. A few years after the great battle at Kadesh, Muwatallis died suddenly and unexpectedly. And one of his sons—Urhi-Teshub—succeeded him as king. Urhi-Teshub proved to be an unpopular ruler. Then, his situation got even worse. A few years later, his uncle, Hattusilis, deposed him in a successful coup (government takeover). The new king took the title of Hattusilis III.

Hittite custom frowned on executing members of the royal family. So Hattusilis banished Urhi-Teshub to Syria. There, out of spite, the young man began having secret dealings with the Babylonians (neighbors of the Assyrians in Mesopotamia). Apparently he wanted to raise an army, defeat his uncle, and thereby regain the throne of Hatti. Hattusilis got wind of what was happening, however, and he drove Urhi-Teshub out of Syria.

It is unclear whether Urhi-Teshub asked Ramesses for asylum (refuge) in Egypt, or whether the pharaoh offered it on his own. What is certain is that Ramesses provided the Hittite nobleman with a comfortable residence. Hattusilis then sent letters to Ramesses, demanding that he return his controversial royal guest. But Ramesses refused. Part of the proof consists of the following passage from a letter Hattusilis wrote to the king of Babylon:

> My enemy [Urhi-Teshub] who fled to another country went to the king of Egypt. I wrote to him [Ramesses], [saying] "Bring my enemy [back to me]." [But] he did not bring my enemy [back]. Then I and the king of Egypt became enemies of one another [even more than we had been before], and to your father [an earlier king of Babylon] I wrote: "The king of Egypt went to help my enemy."[4]

Exactly what happened to Urhi-Teshub after Ramesses took him in remains a mystery to this day. Some scholars think that the pharaoh allowed him to live in Egypt for the rest of his days. If so, Ramesses may have viewed his guest as a sort of ace in the hole in his relations with the Hittites. In other words, if need be, Ramesses could offer to back Urhi-Teshub in a bid to regain Hatti's throne. Other scholars take Ramesses at his word in a later letter he wrote to Hattusilis. In this document, the pharaoh claimed that Urhi-Teshub had left Egypt for parts unknown. "Look," the letter reads in part, "I don't understand these words you have written about this matter of Urhi-Teshub. . . . I do not know where he is lodged. [He has flown away like a bird.]"[5]

A Peace Offering

Wherever Urhi-Teshub really was, Hattusilis was sure he was still at Ramesses' court. And this was a considerable embarrassment to the Hittite king. Also, Hattusilis recognized, as Ramesses did, the possibility that Ramesses might provide Urhi-Teshub with military aid. At some point, Hattusilis realized that there was a way he might keep this from happening. In short, he could make peace with Ramesses. After all, if Egypt and Hatti were allies, Ramesses would be far less likely to become involved in an anti-Hittite plot.

As Bryce and other experts on ancient Hittite affairs point out, another motive for making peace with Ramesses was to increase Hattusilis' personal prestige. Ever since he had deposed Urhi-Teshub, other Near Eastern rulers had scorned the new Hittite leader. In their eyes he was not the rightful king of Hatti. Signing a major treaty with the king of Egypt, Hattusilis believed, would confirm him as the legitimate king of Hatti. It would also establish him as a major player in Near Eastern political affairs. "Most important from Hattusilis' point of view," Bryce writes, "was the fact that the treaty provided him with [unquestioned] acknowledgment of the legitimacy [legality] of his reign."[6]

With all of this and maybe more in mind, Hattusilis made the first move in the peacemaking process. In the twenty-first year of Ramesses' reign (about 1259 or 1258 B.C.), the Hittite ruler sent two special ambassadors to Egypt. The surviving Egyptian record of these events names these men as Tesub and Rhamose and states:

> There came [to Egypt] the royal envoy [ambassador or messenger] . . . of the land of Hatti . . . Tesub, [along with] the second envoy of Hatti, [named] Rhamose . . . to request peace from the Majesty of the king of Upper and Lower Egypt [Ramesses] . . . the Bull of Rulers, who has set his boundaries wherever he wished, in any land.[7]

The ambassadors proposed not only that Egypt and Hatti should end their long hostilities, but that they should become allies as well.

The ball was now in Ramesses' court, so to speak. He could throw the ambassadors out and continue the long struggle with the Hittites. Or he could welcome the opportunity to become Hattusilis' friend. The main question in the pharaoh's mind had to be: What incentives did he have for negotiating a treaty? Bryce speculates about what Ramesses was thinking at the time the ambassadors' visit:

> His campaigns [in Syria] had tapered off considerably in recent years. And any ambitions he had originally entertained [in that region] were now, he had to acknowledge, completely [hopeless]. He had not even been able to recover former Egyptian territories lost to the Hittites in the aftermath of the battle of Kadesh. . . . It is [also] possible that the growing power of Assyria was a factor in Ramesses' decision. . . . [In addition] Ramesses was now two decades into his reign, and may

have felt the need for some significant achievement in the international arena to bolster his image among his subjects. In the absence of any significant military triumphs abroad in recent years, perhaps the next best thing was a major diplomatic achievement. . . . [The treaty and alliance] provided good propaganda value for the pharaoh.[8]

PROMISES OF NONAGGRESSION AND MUTUAL AID

Having weighed the benefits and consequences of the alliance with Hatti. Ramesses decided to go ahead with it. Likely aided by his vizier (chief civilian administrator and advisor) and other advisors, he negotiated an agreement with the Hittite ambassadors. Two copies of the treaty have survived. The original was inscribed on silver tablets. But these disappeared in later ancient times. An Egyptian copy was written on a temple wall at Karnak. And a Hittite copy was carved on clay tablets that modern archaeologists found in the ruins of the Hittite capital, Hattusa (now called Bogazkale).

The first section of the treaty contains general statements proclaiming peace between the two parties. "Behold," it begins, "Hattusilis, the great chief of Hatti, has made himself [to enter] in[to] a treaty with Ramesses, the great ruler of Egypt." There would be brotherhood between the two men "forever." Moreover, their children would remain "in brotherhood and at peace." Thus, the two nations "shall be at peace and in brotherhood like us forever. And hostilities shall not be made between them forever."[9]

After these initial friendly formalities, the treaty spells out a series of promises each side made to the other. First is a nonaggression pact. Ramesses vowed never to "trespass into the land of Hatti."[10] And Hattusilis promised never to invade Egypt. In and of itself, this provision was more or less another formality. Both kings knew that it was highly unlikely that either would ever launch a full-scale invasion of the other's homeland.

Much more meaningful and important was a provision about mutual defense. Each side vowed to help the other if a third party attacked it. The provision reads:

> If another enemy comes to the lands of [Ramesses], the great ruler of Egypt, and he sends to the great chief of Hatti, saying, "Come with me as help against him [the invading third party]," the great chief of Hatti shall come to him [the Egyptian pharaoh], [and] the great chief of Hatti shall slay [the pharaoh's enemy]. . . . Or if Ramesses, the great ruler of Egypt, becomes incensed [angry] against servants of his, and they do another offense against him, and he goes to slay his enemies, the great chief of Hatti shall act with him to destroy everyone against whom they [the Egyptian and Hittite kings] shall be incensed.[11]

WITNESSED BY THE GODS

Another extraordinary provision of the treaty between Ramesses and Hattusilis dealt with the treatment of fugitives from one or the other nation. Part of it reads: "If any great man flee from the land of Egypt and he comes to the lands of the great chief of Hatti . . . the great chief of Hatti shall not receive [him]."[12] Moreover, the Hittite king would place the fugitive in custody and deliver him to the Egyptian pharaoh. (The pharaoh promised to do the same in the case of a Hittite fugitive who ended up in Egypt.)

In pressing for this provision, Hattusilis obviously wanted to avoid any further situations like the one with Urhi-Teshub. The Hittite king realized that it was too late now for him to get his errant nephew back. The treaty covered only those people who became fugitives after the document was signed. However, from now on each party would be forbidden from giving asylum to domestic enemies of the other.

The final provision of the treaty stated what would happen if either party broke the agreement. It was obvious that such an event would plunge Egypt and Hatti back into a state of mutual distrust and war. So this reality remained unstated. In its place, the parties to the treaty called on the gods to witness the document. The parties to the treaty asked the gods to pledge divine vengeance on the nation that breached the agreement. "A thousand gods of the land of Hatti and a thousand gods of the land of Egypt shall destroy" the house, land, and servants of the treaty-breaker, the provision stated. On the other hand, if the two parties upheld the treaty, the same gods would cause both "to be healthy and to live [in prosperity]."[13]

This carving on the wall of the Temple of Amon at Karnak shows
Ramesses bowing before the god Amon-Ra.

His Policies Written in Stone

Whether or not they were motivated by fear of divine punishment, neither Ramesses nor Hattusilis broke the treaty. In fact, both sides celebrated the agreement. They exchanged gifts and pleasant letters and overall did their best to foster friendship between the two empires. Kenneth Kitchen, a leading authority on Ramesses, summarizes some of the cultural exchanges between the two nations following the pact:

> The occasion of the signing of the treaty was one of official rejoicing, and messages of congratulation and good wishes passed between the two royal courts of Egypt and Hatti. And [this was] not merely between the two kings as signatories [signers] of the treaty. In Hatti . . . when her husband [Hattusilis] sent greetings to Ramesses, Queen Pudukhepa wrote a parallel [similar] letter of greeting to Queen Nefertari, still Ramesses' principal consort [at that time]. . . . From Egypt, alongside Ramesses himself, his mother . . . Tuya, sent a letter of greetings to Hatti, as did the . . . [Egyptian] vizier, Paser. . . . [Also] by way of practical and visible evidence of the new cordiality [friendly relations], the two courts exchanged presents—Nefertari sent jewels, dyed [fabrics], and royal garments to her "sister" [Queen Pudukhepa]. . . . So the new relationship [between the two countries] got underway to a promising start.[14]

In addition, these good relations eventually resulted in Ramesses' marriages to two Hittite princesses.

It is also significant that none of Ramesses' successors broke the treaty. Egypt and Hatti, once bitter

DIVINE WITNESSES FOR THE TREATY

The conclusion of the peace treaty between Ramesses and Hattusilis contains the following provision calling on the gods to witness the document and punish the party that violates it. (The translation is by A.H. Gardiner, in a 1920 article in the *Journal of Egyptian Archaeology*.)

> As for these words of the treaty made by the great chief of Hatti with Ramesses, the great ruler of Egypt, in writing upon this tablet of silver . . . a thousand gods, male gods and female gods of those of the land of Hatti, together with a thousand gods . . . of those of the land of Egypt—they are with me as witnesses hearing these words. . . . As to these words . . . [and] as to him who shall not keep them, a thousand gods of the land of Hatti and a thousand gods of the land of Egypt shall destroy his house, his land, and his servants. But he who shall keep these words . . . by they Hatti or be they Egyptians . . . a thousand gods of the land of Hatti and a thousand gods of the land of Egypt will cause him to be healthy and to live, together with his houses and his land and his servants.[15]

enemies, remained allies until the Hittite empire fell apart in the twelfth century B.C. (The causes of this event were unrelated to Egypt.) It is a testament to Ramesses' larger-than-life reputation that later pharaohs honored the great peace he and Hattusilis had made. Egyptians in the generations immediately following Ramesses looked back at him as a leader of uncommon wisdom and valor. And his laws, policies, and treaties seemed truly written in stone.

A GREAT BUILDER

Although Ramesses earned a reputation as an outstanding warrior-pharaoh, his military exploits were not his only claim to fame. The Egyptians of his day and of later generations also saw him as a spectacular builder. Indeed, some felt he was the greatest builder Egypt had ever seen. And many modern observers agree. As Egypt's leading archaeologist, Zahi Hawass, puts it:

> [Ramesses] left behind a legacy of monuments unequalled by any other pharaoh of the New Kingdom. No site in Egypt was untouched by his builders and his monuments. His temples, chapels, statues, and stelae can be found throughout the country. . . . [In fact] it is amazing how much building activity was carried out by this king.[1]

Many of these structures and other artifacts have survived in varying degrees of preservation. For convenience, they can be divided into two general categories. The first includes those buildings or other monuments that were additions to or repairs of older structures. The second category consists of those that Ramesses created from scratch.

These building projects did more than glorify the pharaoh and beautify the country. They also had a unifying effect on the Egyptian people. Whether an addition or a completely new structure, each project employed hundreds and sometimes thousands of workers. (With occasional minor exceptions, the workers were not slaves, as often depicted in movies. Instead, they were mainly farmers who worked as construction workers in their off-season, between planting and the harvest.) There were many dozens of projects spread across the length and breadth of Egypt, as well as in Nubia, during Ramesses' reign. So it is possible that at least a few people from almost every town in the country built something for Ramesses at one time or another. This must have made many Egyptians feel as if they had a personal connection with Ramesses. They could tell their grandchildren that they had worked for a man then widely viewed as the greatest ruler in history.

THE GREAT HALL AT KARNAK

Of the first category of Ramesses' building projects—additions to existing structures—one of the most striking was the great hall at Karnak. Located on the Nile's east bank near the city of Thebes, Karnak consisted of an immense complex of temples. Most of them honored Amun-Ra, the leading deity worshiped in the New Kingdom. Each New Kingdom pharaoh felt obliged to make some contribution to the complex, which grew larger and larger over the centuries. Some pharaohs erected new pylons (large ceremonial gateways) and/or obelisks (tall stone towers with pyramid-shaped tops). Others constructed pillar-lined halls. Or they erected large statues of gods or sphinxes (mythical creatures with the body of a lion and the head of a person).

Ramesses contributed all of these kinds of structures to the Karnak complex. For example, he added 120 stone sphinxes to those already lining a ceremonial avenue. This sacred way linked the Karnak complex to the great Luxor temple, almost two miles to the south. Ramesses also added a new pylon at Karnak, today called the Second Pylon.

EUROPEANS AWED BY KARNAK'S RUINS

The ruins of the Karnak temple complex and Luxor temple cover well more than half a square mile. David Roberts, a gifted Scottish painter, visited these sites in 1838 and painted many aspects of them. Later, in his diary, he commented about the awe-inspiring aspects of these mighty ruins:

> You have to . . . walk among these gigantic structures to understand [their true immensity]. . . . The columns are over 30 feet in circumference, so that a man looks tiny beside them. The blocks that lie scattered all around are so huge that, even without considering how they were cut, it is impossible to imagine how they were brought here and put in their places.[2]

Ramesses' most splendid addition to Karnak, however, was his massive hypostyle hall. The term "hypostyle" comes from Greek words meaning "resting on pillars." A hypostyle hall, a common feature of Egyptian temple architecture, was a covered courtyard in which the roof was held up by rows of columns. These pillars filled most of the chamber. In contrast, most of the columns in a Greek or Roman temple stood along its perimeter. The hall had been initiated by Ramesses I (although some scholars think its construction may have begun under earlier pharaohs). Later, Seti I had continued its construction.

Seti's son, Ramesses II, decided to finish the great hall. In its final form, it featured 134 columns arranged in 16 rows. The twelve columns in the two middle rows stand an astounding seventy-nine feet high, while the pillars in the outer rows are each forty feet high. Ramesses ordered his workmen and artists to decorate the walls of the hall with reliefs and inscriptions. The outer walls held elaborate depictions of his great Kadesh campaign. Among the scenes adorning the interior walls was one showing Ramesses' coronation (crowning ceremony).

THE LUXOR TEMPLE

Ramesses' additions to the nearby Luxor temple, which he began in the third year of his reign, were equally impressive. This temple, also the work of several pharaohs, was the central focus of one of Egypt's most important annual religious festivals. Known as the

Festival of Opet, it featured a grand procession of priests and high officials. As thousands of worshippers watched, prayed, and chanted, the marchers carried stone images of various gods and pharaohs. They carted these statues along the sphinx-lined avenue leading from Karnak to Luxor.

Ramesses erected two huge pylons in the front section of the Luxor temple. On these he had his artists create another set of reliefs depicting his supposed overwhelming victory over the Hittites at Kadesh. The pylons were flanked by two giant statues of Ramesses. Also located out front were two towering obelisks made of red granite. (One still stands in its original position. The French removed the other in 1835 and transported it to the Place de la Concorde in Paris.)

A number of columns line the courtyard of the Luxor temple.

The pylons opened into a large inner courtyard. In addition to seventy-four columns lining the perimeter, the courtyard featured more huge statues of Ramesses. The walls were decorated with scenes showing the pharaoh and his wife Nefertari meeting with various gods. One relief shows the queen shaking a *sistrum* (a musical instrument that made a rattling sound) and praying for her husband's well-being. An accompanying inscription gives the text of the prayer:

> Playing the *sistra* before your beautiful face, I sing of love. . . . I play the *sistra* before your beautiful face. I propitiate [appease] you for your goodness sake. May you protect your son, whom you love, and with whom you are pleased. The Lord of the two lands [Upper and Lower Egypt], [Ramesses], given life like Ra, eternally.[3]

THE RAMESSEUM

The Karnak complex and Luxor temple were not the only sites in the area of Thebes in which Ramesses left his mark as a builder. Across the Nile from Luxor, early in his reign the young pharaoh began work on his mortuary temple. Actually, Ramesses eventually built several mortuary temples for himself in various parts of the country. However, this one, near Thebes and close to his tomb in the Valley of the Kings, remained the most important. The pharaoh and those he knew called it "The Mansion of Millions of Years, United-with-Thebes." In modern times, the structure became known as the Ramesseum.

Preparing for Death While Still Alive

It was not uncommon for pharaohs to start their tombs and mortuary temples while still young. First, these structures were very big and took a long time to complete. Second, life expectancy was then much shorter than it is today. So it was possible a pharaoh might die young. Ramesses wanted the structures that would serve him in the afterlife to be ready in case that happened.

The Ramesseum is one of the few buildings of ancient Egypt for which the name of the architect is known. He was called Penre. Virtually nothing else is known about him except that he designed one of the most impressive structures of the ancient world. The front of the temple featured an enormous pylon. Like Ramesses' other pylons, this one was decorated with scenes of his military triumphs. Directly behind the pylon sprawled two huge open-air courtyards. The first courtyard was at ground level, while a stone ramp led up to the raised second courtyard. Both of these yards were dominated by large statues of the pharaoh. Walking farther into the complex, one reached a magnificent hypostyle hall with a forest of forty-eight towering columns. Finally came a small but richly decorated chamber. This was the holy-of-holies—the room in which Ramesses' priests would pray for the well-being of his soul following his death.

Like other large-scale Egyptian mortuary temples, the Ramesseum had numerous other supporting

The Ramesseum in Egypt is a huge structure. Here, a man standing on a broken statue looks tiny in comparison to the ruins around him.

elements lining the big central courtyards and halls. "To the south of the first court," Joyce Tyldesley writes,

> and connected to it by a gateway, was a small palace. [It featured an] audience chamber, throne room, and balcony (or "window of appearances"), which allowed the palace to communicate with the temple. Here the king and his court could live while visiting Thebes for the celebration of the many local festivals. A double shrine, dedicated jointly to the queen mother Tuya and queen consort Nefertari, was to be found to the north of the hypostyle hall. [Mean]while, the temple proper was surrounded by mud-brick subsidiary buildings such as administrative offices and accommodation provided for

The Impermanence of Human Works

In the 1800s, a number of Europeans visited the Ramesseum and were awed by the majesty of its ruins. One of them, English poet Percy Shelley, was moved to write his now famous poem "Ozymandias." (This ancient name was a misspelling of Ramesses' praenomen.) The words beautifully capture the fragility and impermanence of all human works, no matter how great at their inception:

And on the pedestal these words appear:
"My name is Ozymandias, king of kings;
Look on my works, ye mighty, and despair!"
Nothing beside remains; round the decay
Of that colossal wreck, boundless and bare,
The lone and level sands stretch far away.[4]

the temple officials. The entire complex was protected by a thick mud-brick wall.[5]

RAMESSES' IMPRESSIVE NEW CITY

In addition to single structures like his mortuary temple, Ramesses constructed an entire city. It stood on the site of a smaller settlement begun by his father, Seti. Ramesses' well-crafted and impressive new city—called Pi-Ramesse—was located near the eastern Nile Delta. Very little remains of the place now. Archaeologists believe that the region it occupied, somewhat east and south of the Nile's Pelusiac branch, was then quite fertile. A nearby lake allowed construction of a port. Ships made their way from the city, through the Delta, and out into the Mediterranean Sea. About Pi-Ramesse, an ancient visitor wrote:

> It is a beautiful place. . . . Life in the residence [of the pharaoh and his nobles] is good. The fields are filled with all kinds of good produce, so that each day is blessed with good food. Its canals team with fish and its marshland is filled with birds. . . . The granaries overflow with barley and wheat.[6]

The words "life in the residence" refer to the fact that Pi-Ramesse was mainly a royal residence. Its central portion consisted of a large compound, perhaps covering an area of four square miles. The main structure in the compound was a magnificent palace. Historian Kenneth Kitchen describes it here, based on various pieces of archaeological and literary evidence:

Within the prim [neat] whitened walls painted pavements probably led between royal apartments and the more public halls of audience ... which glittered with splendid glazed tiles. These glowed with warm, rich colors—yellows and browns, a touch of blue, red, and black, with gray backgrounds. Thus adorned, the steps and dais [platform] for the royal throne had figures of subject foreigners over a [painted scene] of marsh plants in blue. . . . Doorways, walls, and balconies had the titles of Ramesses in bold hieroglyphics [picture-signs], white-on-blue and blue-on-white, and triumphal scenes [of the pharaoh's military victories] vivid in red, blue, brown, yellow, and black. Within the more intimate royal apartments, this official bombast [overly grand and flowery displays] gave way to happier [and more intimate] scenes—of birds and animals in the marshes, ladies of the harem, and Bes, the comic little god of hearth and home.[7]

Clustered around the palace were other impressive buildings and displays. These included a treasury, quarters for Ramesses' harem, administrative offices, religious temples, and military barracks. There were also shops for royal artisans, extensive gardens, and even a royal zoo. Cheaper housing for artisans, farmers, and laborers surrounded the compound. Many of the workers who lived in the city were among those who had built it. A surviving inscription, dating from 1272 B.C., shows that the pharaoh struck a deal with these workers. He praised them lavishly and then agreed to feed and clothe them extremely well if they would work hard for him. "You chosen workmen," the inscription begins, valiant men of proven skill . . . craftsmen in valuable stone, experienced in [working with] granite . . . good fellows, tireless and vigilant [watchful] at work all day, who execute their tasks with energy and ability! . . . Abundant provisions [piles of supplies are laid out] before you. . . . I am your constant provider. The supplies assigned for you are weightier [worth more] than the work, in my desire to [generously] nourish and foster you! I know your labors to be eager and able, and that work is only a pleasure with a full stomach. The granaries [storage bins for grain] grown with grain for you. I have filled the stores for you with everything [you could ever need]—with bread, meat, cakes . . . sandals, clothing, enough [palm oil] for anointing your heads [to be] issued every ten days. . . . None of you need [to] pass the night moaning about poverty![8]

The labors of these workers were certainly impressive. The glittering city of Pi-Ramesse was a proud showpiece of Ramesses' reign. However, it was not fated to retain its prominence for very long. By the close of the New Kingdom (ca. 1069 B.C.), the city had greatly diminished in importance. Builders had begun to use its stones for newer structures in other cities, and nature also took a toll. Later in ancient times, the Pelusiac branch of the Nile River shifted position, leaving the city isolated. The region around it then rapidly became arid. So the city was abandoned and over time most of it rotted away or was buried by sand.

THE TEMPLES AT ABU SIMBEL

Each of Ramesses' many temples, palaces, and other structures was imposing and splendid, to be sure. This was true of the buildings both inside and outside of the city of Pi-Ramesse. Yet all of these works paled in comparison to what came to be seen as the single-greatest building Ramesses ever had built. This was the great temple at Abu Simbel, on the Nile's west bank in northern Nubia. The temple was unusual in a number of ways. First, it was set in a very remote area. Ramesses chose the spot, as well as the particular angle and positioning of the structure, to create a specific and spectacular effect. Twice a year (on February 20 and October 20), the rising sun would shine directly through the building's front entrance. The rays would illuminate four sacred statues situated deep inside the temple.

Another unusual aspect of the great Abu Simbel temple was the manner in which it was constructed. It was not built in the standard way, by stacking thousands of quarried stones. Rather, workmen painstakingly carved the temple from the face of a massive cliff overlooking the Nile. The cliff was made of pink-tinted stone that became even more beautiful when struck by the rays of the rising sun. The front, or façade, was cut into the shape of an immense pylon. "Steps lead up to a ledge decorated with sculptures of falcons as symbols of the sun god," writes Hawass. (Hawass had complete charge of the Abu Simbel site in the 1970s and knows its every detail.)

This ledge extends across the façade of the temple in front of four colossal [gigantic] seated figures of Ramesses. . . . All four statues show Ramesses seated with his hands flat on his knees, bare-chested, and wearing a royal kilt, with a *nemes* headdress and the double crown of united Egypt on his head. Standing at the feet of these statues are images of eleven members of the king's family.

About the interior of the temple, Hawass first describes the entrance:

[It] leads to a corridor whose walls are engraved with images of Ramesses presenting sacrificial plates to [the gods]. . . . On the columns to the left as one enters the hall, Ramesses carved . . . the following figures: On the first, the king burns incense before an image of himself as a god; on the second, Queen Nefertari burns incense. . . . On the third, the king presents flowers to [the gods]. . . . The ceiling between the two lines of columns is decorated with an image of the vulture goddess Nekhbet spreading her wings; the two sides of the ceiling are decorated with stars. The eastern wall is dominated by a drawing of the king with eight of his sons smiting [striking] Nubian and Hittite prisoners in the presence of the god Amun. . . . Doors in the northern wall of the hall open into rooms that appear to have been used as storerooms. . . . In the center of the western wall . . . is a doorway leading to a second, smaller room . . . [whose] walls and columns [are] decorated with religious scenes.[9]

This second hall leads to a third hall. And the third one opens into an inner sanctuary. It was in this inner chamber that priests conducted the principal religious

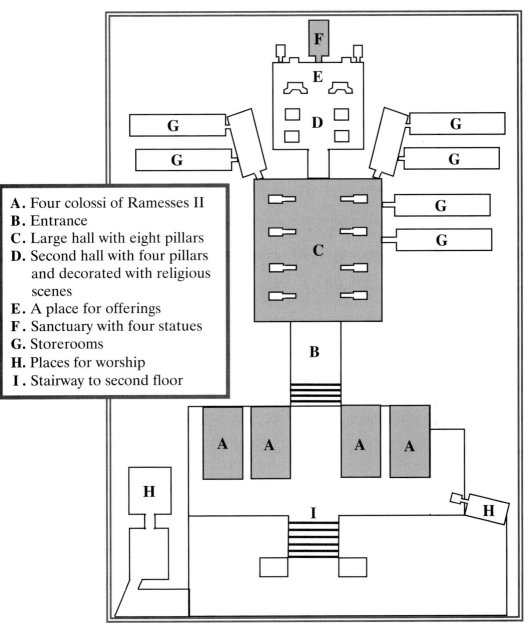

A. Four colossi of Ramesses II
B. Entrance
C. Large hall with eight pillars
D. Second hall with four pillars and decorated with religious scenes
E. A place for offerings
F. Sanctuary with four statues
G. Storerooms
H. Places for worship
I. Stairway to second floor

A map of the temple at Abu Simbel

sacrifices. The chamber lies a full 160 feet back inside the cliff from the front entrance. Carving out these inner corridors and rooms—not to mention decorating them so elaborately—were clearly engineering and artistic feats of the highest order.

Not far from the great temple, Ramesses ordered the construction of a second, smaller one. This one extended back into the cliffs about half as far as the inner chambers of the larger temple did—about eighty feet. The smaller structure was built for Nefertari. The structure also honored the goddess Hathor, whom the queen had chosen as her personal patron deity. Outside the temples stood six large statues. Two were of Nefertari herself and four were of Ramesses. Smaller statues of their children were also erected.

Ramesses began work on the Abu Simbel temples fairly early in his reign. He dedicated them in his twenty-fourth regnal year (ca. 1253 B.C.), although they may not have been fully completed until a few years later. Actually, the pharaoh was fortunate that he was able to finish them at all. Archaeologists have determined that in Ramesses' thirtieth or perhaps thirty-first regnal year a large earthquake struck the region of Abu Simbel. Nefertari's temple came through with only minor cracks. But the great temple suffered considerable damage. Inside, in the temple's great hall, most of the pillars cracked. Some tilted to one side and one came crashing down. Meanwhile, one of the four huge statues of the pharaoh gracing the façade lost an arm. And the entire upper half of another collapsed. Repairs were undertaken at once. According to Kitchen, Ramesses' vizier, Paser,

> immediately took in hand repairs with all speed, probably sending word to the king (in the capital, a thousand miles to the north) as soon as his efforts seemed to have some chance of succeeding. Thus the pillars of the great hall were shored up with masonry . . . and the collapsed pillar rebuilt and restored. The doorjamb was rebuilt but left plain, while the fallen south arm of the [big statue] north of the entranceway was restored.[10]

However, the statue whose upper sections had collapsed could not be repaired. And it never fully recovered. "Here," Kitchen continues, "all Paser could do was to tidy up, leaving the major parts where they had fallen (nor has anyone done any better since)."[11] Thus, sadly for Ramesses, within his own lifetime his single greatest creation was already in a state of partial ruin.

Nature then continued the process of decay. Several generations following Ramesses' passing, the temple's priests finally abandoned the site. Soon afterward, sand began to bury it. And by late medieval times, it had almost totally disappeared from view. Eventually, modern archaeologists excavated it. But then came a new threat. In the 1960s it looked as if the great temple would be submerged under an artificial lake created by a new dam. Many people around the world could not bear the thought of such a great historical treasure being lost forever. So an international rescue effort of epic proportions took shape. Archaeologists and engineers carefully

SAVING THE ABU SIMBEL TEMPLES

One of history's greatest salvage operations was finished in the 1960s. In the late 1950s, the Egyptian government decided to build a huge new dam at Aswan (long ago in Nubia but now in southern Egypt). The purpose was to control the yearly flooding cycle of the Nile River. Installing the dam would create a new waterway—Lake Nasser—315 miles long and 16 miles wide. The problem was that this new lake would submerge the remains of Ramesses II's great temples at Abu Simbel. In an effort to save these priceless monuments, the United Nations agency UNESCO became involved.

UNESCO officials coordinated a world-wide rescue project. Engineers cut the larger temple into 807 pieces, each weighing from 3 to 20 tons. Nefertari's temple was cut into 225 pieces. An artificial hill duplicating the original one that held the temples was created on safe ground high above the new lake. There, all the pieces were reassembled in 1967. The operation was so well planned and executed that many people thought the structures looked as if they had never been moved at all.

cut the monument into pieces and reassembled it at a safe location on higher ground.

Building Ramesses' Colossi

Today, scholars refer to large statues like those fronting the Abu Simbel temples as colossi (from the word colossal, meaning huge). The four that sat outside the larger temple were seventy-two feet high. Their weights have never been calculated with certainty. However, scholars agree that each would tip the scales (if one could find scales big enough!) at a minimum of 3 million pounds.

The great size of these colossi was not the only thing about them that was unusual when they were constructed. Because they were carved in place from existing rock formations, they never had to be moved to their final location. (The Great Sphinx, near the pyramids at Giza, is another example of a colossus carved in place.) In contrast, most of Ramesses' other colossi (and those of other pharaohs) did have to be transported to their final sites. And this required an enormous outlay of time, skill, and sheer muscle power.

Each of Ramesses' transported colossi began as a huge slab or lump of stone in a distant quarry. The stone ranged from relatively soft varieties, like limestone and sandstone, to harder ones like granite and basalt. The sculptors typically selected a slab that was a little larger than the finished statue would be. This would allow them to remove material when carving the colossus.

At the front of the temple of Abu Simbel are four colossi (inset). These are huge statues of Ramesses, each over sixty feet high. A close-up of two of the statues appears in the larger photo.

First, the sculptors painted outlines of the figure directly onto the front, back, and sides of the slab. The outlines acted as a guide to show the workmen where to cut into the stone. The sculptors then chipped away the stone a little at a time. They did this until they had created a figure that approximated the overall shape of the desired statue. Then they painted various dots and lines on the rough form to make new guidelines. Using stone hammers and metal chisels, they carefully chipped away more stone, expertly modeling the face, body, clothes, headdress, and so forth. The final product was sanded and polished. And eyes made of white and black stones were inlaid and painted.

In fact, it was considered extremely important for such a colossus to appear lifelike. The numerous statues of Ramesses erected across Egypt were not merely standardized sculptures with generic features. They were instead partial portraits of the pharaoh himself. The reasons for this artistic custom were rooted in Egypt's most ancient and cherished religious beliefs. Most statues in temples, whether large or small, were viewed as host vehicles. These were refuges for nonphysical spirits or beings. Such a being might be the spirit of a god or goddess. Or it might be the soul of a dead pharaoh or other human. The basic belief was that the spirit rested for a while inside the statue and from there could communicate with the living. In her book about Egyptian statues, Gay Robins writes that:

> [such statues] were places where a non-physical entity—a deity, the [soul of the king], or the [souls] of the dead—

could manifest [exist, or live] in this world. The statue provided a physical body and had to be recognizable and appropriate to the being that was meant to manifest in it. Since such beings were not physical entities, they were unrestricted by time and space and could be simultaneously present in all their [sculpted] images wherever they were located.[12]

Thus, if the statue did not look like the god or person it represented, it would be seen as unsuitable. The invisible entity would refuse to inhabit it. For this reason, most of the surviving statues of Ramesses likely look fairly close to the way he did in life.

Moving the Colossi

This idea of a statue as a vessel for one's soul explains in part why Ramesses erected so many well-crafted statues of himself, including many colossi, across his country. He hoped that after he died and entered the afterlife, he would be able to return to Earth. And from the interiors of his widely-placed statues, he would be able gaze on his ancestral lands and his descendants forever.

Of these royal images, many were constructed for the Ramesseum. The biggest colossus at the temple towered to a height of sixty-two feet and weighed an astounding one thousand tons. This is somewhat smaller than the four largest Abu Simbel giants. But one must keep in mind that this one had to be quarried, transported overland, and then raised into a standing position.

A Roman View of Ramesses' Obelisk

This ancient description of one of the obelisks erected by Ramesses II was penned by the first-century A.D. Roman scholar Pliny the Elder in his encyclopedia-like *Natural History*. Many centuries separated Ramesses from Pliny. So the Roman had few facts to go on. And he vastly exaggerated the number of workers involved. The completely unfounded tale about the pharaoh's son was based on a fable that had become widespread by Pliny's day.

> [The obelisk] is 200 feet in height and is extraordinarily thick, each side being 17 feet in width. Some 120,000 men are said to have carried out this work. When the obelisk was about to be set upright, the king himself was afraid that the lifting equipment would not be strong enough to take the weight. To make his workmen pay attention to the dangers, he tied his son to the top, so that in ensuring the child's safety the work-force would treat the monolith with necessary care.[13]

The manner in which this was accomplished shows the great ingenuity of ancient Egyptian builders. One might suppose that it took enormous numbers of laborers to drag such a heavy statue. But in fact, the number of workers involved was fairly small considering the immense size of the task. Archaeologists have found tomb paintings showing the moving of colossi. At the quarry, such a statue was loaded onto a wooden sledge, which resembled a larger version of a modern sled. One worker stood on the front of the sledge and poured a liquid (perhaps palm oil or milk) in front of it as it moved along. The liquid significantly reduced the friction of the sledge against the wooden rollers or tracks over which it was dragged. Therefore, a single worker was able to drag about a third of a ton. Using this ratio, one can calculate that 172 men could drag a 58-ton statue. And a 700-ton colossus could be moved by just 2,100 laborers. This was a workforce that Ramesses could have raised easily at any time and on short notice.

This was the way the great colossus at the Ramesseum reached its final resting place. It remained in place, a true wonder of the world, for several generations. But a few centuries after Ramesses' death its upper section collapsed in an earthquake. The great head then rested on the ground for ages to come until modern Europeans first saw it. Among them was the renowned nineteenth-century English poet Percy Bysshe Shelley. On seeing the fallen giant, he was inspired to write his now famous poem "Ozymandias." It reads in part:

> *Two vast and trunkless legs of stone*
> *stand in the desert. Near them on the sand,*
> *half sunk, a shattered visage [face] lies, whose frown*
> *and wrinkled lip and sneer of cold command*
> *tell that its sculptor well those passions read*[14]

Incredibly, Ramesses' colossus at the Ramesseum was surpassed in size by other transportable statues of that pharaoh. Four unfinished giant images of him, now in fragments, still rest in a quarry. If they had been finished and raised upright, each would have reached a height of close to eighty feet. And each would have weighed more than one thousand tons. Even in their ruined state, they continue to serve one of their major original functions. This is to keep the name of their illustrious creator—Egypt's greatest builder—alive for all eternity.

8

FINAL YEARS, DEATH, AND LEGACY

One of the reasons that Ramesses accomplished so much in his reign was that he ruled for a very long time. In fact, his was one of the longest reigns of any Egyptian pharaoh—a total of some sixty-six years. This gave Ramesses plenty of time to engage in numerous military campaigns. He also had time to have many children and to erect seemingly countless buildings and other monuments throughout Egypt.

Perhaps the most amazing thing about this huge output of activity was how fast it occurred. Indeed, most of it took place in only the first half of Ramesses' reign. For him, the second half was largely quiet and uneventful. For one thing, he had made peace with the Hittites. So Egypt's number-one enemy had become a trusted ally. Also, the pharaoh's ambitious and energetic flurry of building activity had already established him as a great ruler in the eyes of his subjects. So there was no discontent or desire to rebel among the people. Happy with Ramesses' rule, they went about their daily tasks and remained productive. As Kenneth Kitchen puts it:

> With no evident foes or wars abroad to drain her resources, and blessed with good Nile floods and sufficient food-crops most years, Egypt bathed in a relaxed, general prosperity. . . . [The country] hummed with busy activity in field, quarry, workshop, state office, and temple alike.[1]

The pharaoh's deteriorating physical condition was another factor that contributed to the slower pace of his later years. The state of medicine and health care in the ancient world was primitive compared to the situation today in developed countries like the United States. On the one hand, most ancients did not live past the age of forty-five or fifty. And those few who did increasingly suffered from a wide variety of ailments associated with aging. Tooth decay, for example, was common. And yanking out rotting teeth was often the only practical remedy. At least by his late fifties and early sixties, Ramesses likely suffered from poor circulation. This and other ailments surely took a toll on his once strong body.

There is no way to confirm Ramesses' exact physical and mental condition in his final years. After all, Egyptian artistic customs dictated that the pharaoh be portrayed as a young, vigorous man no matter how old and feeble he became. But Ramesses lived well into his nineties. (Since the date of his birth is unknown, his exact age when he died is uncertain). Divine connections or

RAMESSES IN THE MOVIES

Ramesses II was brought to life for the masses in a series of Hollywood films made in the twentieth century. His character was particularly prominent in director Cecil B. DeMille's two versions of *The Ten Commandments* (released in 1923 and 1956 respectively). Actor Charles De Roche played Ramesses in the 1923 version; while the great Yul Brynner portrayed him in the later film. In both versions, Ramesses is presented unflatteringly, and probably inaccurately, as a curt, conceited, self-absorbed ruler who cares little for his people.

Ramesses was also portrayed as a cruel pharaoh in the 1998 Disney animated feature, *The Prince of Egypt*. In this film, the pharaoh's voice was provided by English actor Ralph Fiennes. Unfortunately for Ramesses, so far no one has made a movie that depicts his historically proven deeds or presents him in a positive light.

not, he simply could not have escaped the natural infirmities of old age.

THE AGING PHARAOH DELEGATES AUTHORITY

It is not surprising, therefore, that as he aged Ramesses assigned more and more of his taxing official duties to younger assistants. This situation is well illustrated by his relationship with his son Merenptah. Slowly but steadily, Ramesses allowed his successor to take over key governmental positions and responsibilities. The exact nature of these duties is unknown. But it is safe to assume that Merenptah took charge of the army and dealt with the chief priests of the major temples. It must be remembered that Merenptah himself was not a young man in this period. When Ramesses reached the age of ninety, his leading son was probably at least sixty. So both men were forced, thanks to their declining physical conditions, to give some of their duties to others.

Who were the men in whom the pharaoh and his son placed so much trust and responsibility? For the most part they were officials appointed either by the aging Seti, before Ramesses ascended the throne, or sons or nephews of these noblemen. The most trusted and outstanding of all was Paser, whom Seti had appointed as vizier. Paser's many important duties included acting as chief judge in civil trials and running the state treasury. He also kept the civil service working smoothly and oversaw tax collection. No less crucial a duty, Paser was in charge of the builders and workmen who prepared the tombs of Seti and Ramesses. In the twenty-seventh year of Ramesses' reign (ca. 1252 B.C.), the busy Paser also became high priest of Amun (the leading religious post in the country). Paser died in Ramesses' thirty-eighth regnal year (ca. 1241 B.C.). He was replaced as vizier by a civil servant named Khay. Khay was later succeeded in the post by another trusted administrator, Neferronpet.

These viziers and other capable administrators ran large sectors of the government for Ramesses in his later years. However, evidence shows that the pharaoh increasingly gave authority to Merenptah. Indeed, as

Kitchen points out, "For the final twelve years of his aged father's reign, Merenptah was the real ruler of the kingdom, virtually pharaoh in all but name."[2]

Some of Ramesses' other trusted advisors had been boyhood friends. One was Asha-Hebsed, who served as an army general under both Seti and Ramesses. Later, Asha-Hebsed worked closely with Ramesses in the royal palace. Another boyhood friend, Ameneminet, started out as Ramesses' personal companion and bodyguard. The pharaoh consistently trusted this man with his life. Ramesses trusted Ameneminet so much, in fact, that he promoted him to the important posts of superintendent of horses and royal ambassador.

Ramesses and Merenptah also relied on a few trusted individuals to oversee the numerous building projects that took place in Ramesses' reign. These overseers were often the sons of older advisors who had retired or died. The younger men typically grew up and received their educations in the palace compounds. One of the most outstanding examples was Setau. Ramesses made him Viceroy (governor) of Nubia, a very important position that included maintaining the great Abu Simbel temples. Setau is one of the few advisors in Ramesses' long reign who left behind specific information about himself. It is contained in an autobiographical inscription on a stele and reads in part:

> I was one whom his Lord [the pharaoh] caused to be instructed [educated] . . . as a ward of the palace. I grew up in the royal abode when I was a youth. When I was a youth I was appointed to be Chief Scribe of the Vizier. I

assessed [kept records of] the entire land with a great scroll, a task I was able to perform. . . . His Majesty promoted me to the [position of] High Steward of Amun. I served as Superintendent of the Treasury and Festival Leader of Amun. . . . My lord again recognized my worth. I was appointed Viceroy of Nubia. I directed serfs in thousands and tens of thousands, and Nubians in hundreds of thousands.[3]

RAMESSES' DEATH AND MUMMIFICATION

It was men like Setau and Paser, along with Merenptah, who kept the wheels of government turning in Ramesses later years. Meanwhile, the pharaoh continued to outlive most of his wives and friends. He even outlived many of his children. Finally, however, as it must for all human beings, the end came for Ramesses. No official records have survived that tell his exact age or the cause of death. Apparently, he simply passed away due to the expected complications of extreme old age. (Modern examinations of his remains seem to confirm this.)

What is more certain is what happened when the news of the pharaoh's death was announced. Following custom, messengers rode from the palace at Pi-Ramesse south to Thebes. There, they informed the keepers of Ramesses' already constructed tomb to begin preparations to receive the body. This included filling the tomb with food, clothing, jewelry, weapons, boats, and hundreds of other objects. It was thought that the pharaoh's spirit would need these things in the afterlife.

It is possible that most of these objects had long been stored in the nearby Ramesseum for safekeeping.

The tomb itself, which modern archaeologists call KV7, is located near the entrance to the Valley of the Kings. It appears to be the largest crypt in the whole valley, with a total area of about eighty-eight hundred square feet. It features numerous separate chambers leading off of three main corridors. Two of the rooms are large pillared halls that had ceremonial uses. One of the halls leads to an small chamber, which itself leads to Ramesses' burial chamber (often called the "Golden Chamber"). There was also a small side room off the burial chamber to hold the king's canopic jars. (It was customary to remove a dead person's internal organs and place them in these jars.) For many days, these corridors and chambers were alive with activity as officials and workmen carried Ramesses' grave goods inside.

While the tomb preparations were in progress near Thebes, far to the north the pharaoh's body was prepared for its long journey in the afterlife. The exact location of the embalming house is unknown. But it must have been somewhere in the Nile Delta near the sea. Modern investigators know this from studies of Ramesses' mummy. They found small traces of sand between the linen bandages in which he was wrapped. Microscopic analysis shows that the sand came from salt water, not fresh water. Therefore, the water in which the bandages were washed came from the sea rather than the Nile.

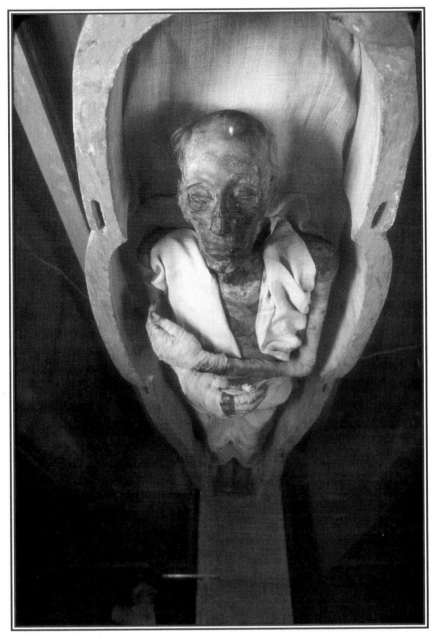

The mummy of Ramesses II has survived for over three thousand years and remains largely intact today. It is currently on display at the Egyptian Museum in Cairo, Egypt.

The mummification process took up to seventy days. After removing the king's internal organs, the embalmers washed his body and packed the empty body cavities with temporary stuffing (to maintain the body's shape). Then they coated the corpse with natron (or natrum), a mineral salt, to help preserve it. After forty days, they took the body to another location. There, the embalmers removed the temporary stuffing and replaced it with linen soaked in resin (plant sap). Finally, they sewed up the larger incisions they had made. They then wrapped the body in strips of fresh linen. Following tradition, appropriate prayers and spells were chanted during each and every stage of the embalming process.

THE FUNERAL

When Ramesses' body was properly prepared, it was time for the funeral. With great pomp and ceremony, family members and government officials bore the pharaoh's body to a royal barge. Tens of thousands of Egyptians, still in a state of intense mourning, likely lined the Nile's banks. Perhaps they chanted prayers and hymns as they watched the boat make its solemn journey upstream toward Thebes.

When the ship reached the docks at that city, priests carried the royal mummy ashore and placed it on a wooden sledge. Again with great pomp and sadness, they dragged the sledge to the Ramesseum. For a period of unknown duration, the body rested there. Almost certainly the temple's priests recited prayers calling on the gods to welcome their earthly representative—the great Ramesses II.

At some point, Merenptah performed the sacred "Opening of the Mouth" ceremony. One by one, the new pharaoh grasped a series of ritual implements—knives and other objects that had been blessed by Ramesses' priests. With each, he touched the eyes, nose, ears, and mouth of the dead man. The Egyptians believed that this ceremony was necessary to ensure that Ramesses' spirit would be able to move and speak in the afterlife. At the conclusion of the ceremony, priests placed the royal corpse in a coffin of solid gold. That coffin nested inside another one, covered with gold leaf and precious jewels. And the second coffin nested within a third, also magnificently decorated. (These coffins have not survived. They were probably stolen by tomb robbers in ancient times. Scholars believe they resembled the ones found in the tomb of "King Tut," one of Ramesses' predecessors.)

The last leg of Ramesses' final journey then began. A huge funeral procession accompanied the nested coffins as a sledge moved them from the Ramesseum to the tomb. Those who marched included the vizier and other high government officials. Also present were the many members of the pharaoh's enormous family. Priests, army generals, and old friends were there, too. In addition, ambassadors from neighboring lands may have attended to pay their respects to a great world leader. As described by Kitchen, the great funeral procession

> formed up, [with] the priests and high officials, the mummy of Ramesses in its coffins on a bier drawn by

oxen, the royal family headed by Merenptah, and a veritable baggage train of attendants. . . . [Leaving the Ramesseum] the long procession went north along the desert edge, turned west along the winding, lonely desert ravine, and so reached at last the Valley of the Kings.[4]

Having reached the tomb, the mourners held a feast in honor of the deceased. Then they carried his coffins down into the waiting crypt. Slowly they moved through the corridors and chambers. It was dark inside so they carried candles and oil lamps to light their way. When they arrived at the burial chamber, they placed the nested coffins in a huge stone coffin and slid the great stone lid in place. Finally, as the mourners departed, some priests swept the chamber clean of dust and soot. Putting out the lamps, they closed and bolted the door. Then the outer door of the tomb was sealed as well and covered with rubble.

 # RAMESSES' IMMEDIATE HEIRS

With the great Ramesses gone, it was up to Merenptah to rule Egypt and maintain the fruits of his father's accomplishments. However, the new pharaoh was not content merely to rest on Ramesses' laurels. Merenptah may have been sixty or more when he took the throne. However, he was neither feeble nor unambitious. Clearly, he wanted to make his own mark on the world and on history.

Unfortunately for Merenptah, making that mark would not be easy. This was because Ramesses had died at a time when the world was rapidly changing. When Ramesses had fought and later made peace with the Hittites, Egypt and Hatti had been the Near East's superpowers. But now, Hatti was in rapid decline. Eventually, it would no longer be strong enough to keep the growing power of Assyria in check.

Merenptah also had to deal with a rising pirate menace from the sea. And he encountered trouble with the Libyans, who had allied themselves with nomadic tribesmen from farther north. To stem a full-fledged invasion of Egypt, Merenptah acted quickly. Probably aided by his son, Prince Seti-Merenptah, he led his army into the western deserts and there soundly defeated the intruders. Merenptah also defeated rebels in both Nubia and Palestine.

Try as he may, though, Merenptah had no chance of matching the achievements of his father. There simply was not enough time. Merenptah died only ten years after ascending the throne (ca. 1203 B.C.). He was succeeded by Amenmessu, who seems to have been one of his lesser sons. (The circumstances of his accession to the throne are unknown. He ruled only three years. Then the crown prince, Seti-Merenptah, took power as Seti II.)

HIS BODY'S LONG JOURNEY

Merenptah was laid to rest in a tomb (now designated KV8) very near that of his father. Unfortunately for both Ramesses and Merenptah, the integrity of their final resting places did not last long. Sometime in the next two centuries thieves broke into and violated the tombs.

THE TOMB OF RAMESSES' SONS

Although the location of Ramesses' tomb was known throughout ancient and modern times, that of his sons did not come to light until recently. In 1825, British scholar James Burton found the lost tomb in the Valley of the Kings. Before it could be properly excavated, however, sand obscured its entrance and it was lost again. The tomb's rediscovery, by American Egyptologist Kent R. Weeks, occurred in 1985.

Called KV5, the tomb originally housed the bodies of more than forty of Ramesses sons and possibly those of other male relatives. It consists of at least 120 rooms, all linked by winding corridors. Along with many mummies, excavators have found canopic jars, statues, jewelry, chariots, clothing, and other grave goods. Weeks and his colleagues are still excavating the tomb and continually find new chambers. They say that the total number may exceed 150. They also estimate that the excavations will require at least two more decades to complete.

Most of the valuables in the tombs, including the magnificent nested coffins, disappeared.

Archaeologists have been able to piece together a rough idea of the long journey that Ramesses' remains now took. After one or more robberies of his tomb, in about 1074 B.C., government officials removed the body, which the tomb robbers had left in the burial chamber. After rebandaging the mummy, the officials placed it in Seti I's tomb (now called KV17). But Seti's tomb was also a target of thieves. So over the course of the following eighty years or so, Ramesses' mummy underwent two more moves. It ended up in the tomb of a high priest named Pinodjem, located at Deir el-Bahari (near the Valley of the Kings). There, priests secretly placed Ramesses' remains alongside those of his father, Ramesses I; Ahmose I; Thutmose III; and other notable New Kingdom pharaohs. Their original tombs had also been violated.

Over time, the location of Pinodjem's tomb was forgotten, even by thieves. So Ramesses II rested in peace for nearly three thousand years. Then, in 1871 a local Egyptian goatherder stumbled onto the concealed entrance to the tomb. Unfortunately, this man was a modern tomb robber. He and members of his family plundered the site for several years before the authorities caught on. The police finally arrested the thieves and safeguarded the tomb. Trained excavators moved the royal mummies to a museum in Cairo.

In the 1880s, scholars at the museum removed the bandages from Ramesses' mummy. They then examined the remains and confirmed that they were indeed those of the man who had fought the Hittites at Kadesh. In the early twentieth century, noted British anatomist Grafton Elliot Smith examined the remains. And in the late 1960s, a more detailed study was made using X-ray analysis. The latter examination showed that the body had badly deteriorated since its unwrapping in the late 1800s. Modern bacteria and fungus had taken a toll on the embalmed skin. Authorities worried that if nothing was done, the pharaoh's remains might rot away beyond repair.

To halt any further decay, in 1975 Egyptian and French officials flew Ramesses' body to a specially prepared medical facility at a museum in Paris. Someone pointed out that he had once been an important head of state. So a French military honor guard greeted and saluted his remains as they were carried from the plane.

In the facility, Ramesses' remains underwent their most intense and sophisticated examination yet, including new X-rays. The exact cause of death was not clear. But the examiners concluded that at some point in his life Ramesses had suffered from ankylosing spondylitis. In this serious medical condition, the bones of the spine fuse together, causing a great deal of pain. (A re-evaluation of these X-rays was performed in the summer of 2004 by Canadian doctors. The results were published in the fall of that year in the *Canadian Association of Radiologists Journal*. The new study suggested that the 1977 diagnosis was incorrect. Instead, of ankylosing spondylitis, the later researchers said, Ramesses suffered from a crippling form of arthritis. It likely began affecting him when he was about fifty years old. Subsequently, the condition caused excessive growth on his vertebrae, or the bones of his spine. This ailment must have kept him in a constant state of pain for the rest of his long life.)

In addition to the physical examination of the mummy performed in 1977, prior damage to the body was repaired at that time. And experts used gamma radiation to sterilize it. In May 1977, Ramesses' mummy was reinstalled in Cairo in a germ- and dust-free display case. It remains there to this day, an attraction that draws tens of thousands of visitors each year.

 ## AN AMBASSADOR FROM THE PAST

Whether they know it or not, these visitors in Cairo are part of Ramesses' great legacy. This is because much of that legacy consists of his own remains and the reverence people have for them thousands of years after his death. His immediate legacy in the years following his passing was a country that was filled with impressive monuments and was at peace with its former enemies. But the effects of these achievements were temporary. Over time, the monuments crumbled. Empires rose and fell. Ramesses' tomb was violated and his mummy disappeared. Meanwhile, memories of him and his deeds became distorted and he steadily became a larger-than-life legend.

Only in the last century or so have experts reexamined Ramesses and restored him to his rightful status as a great national leader. In a sense, he has become a modern ambassador from Egypt's past. Though his eyes and lips are forever shut, his remains speak volumes. They help to focus fresh attention on his incredible personal story and the magnificent civilization of which he was a great leader. Ramesses II continues to serve his beloved Egypt, and humankind, in ways that he could not have imagined when he was alive.

CHRONOLOGY

CA. 3100 B.C.—The first pharaoh, Menes, unites the kingdoms of Upper and Lower Egypt, creating the world's first territorial state.

CA. 2686–2181 B.C.—Egypt's Old Kingdom.

CA. 2055–1650 B.C.—Egypt's Middle Kingdom.

CA. 1650–1550 B.C.—Egypt's Second Intermediate Period, also called the "Hyksos" period, named after a foreign people who invaded and occupied Egypt during this era.

CA. 1550–1069 B.C.—Egypt's New Kingdom.

CA. 1295 B.C.—Ramesses I, grandfather of Ramesses II, ascends the throne of Egypt.

CA. 1294 B.C.—Ramesses I dies and his son, Seti, becomes pharaoh.

CA. 1288 B.C.—Seti's son Ramesses accompanies his father on a military campaign.

CA. 1279 B.C.—Ramesses II succeeds his father as pharaoh.

CA. 1274 B.C.—Ramesses fights the Hittites near the Syrian town of Kadesh.

CA. 1258 B.C.—Ramesses concludes a peace treaty with Hattusilis III, king of the Hittites.

CA. 1255 B.C.—Ramesses' chief and favorite wife, Nefertari, dies.

CA. 1244 B.C.—Ramesses completes the two great temples at Abu Simbel, in Nubia.

CA. 1213 B.C.—Ramesses dies in his nineties and is succeeded by his son Merenptah.

CA. 1203 B.C.—Merenptah dies and is succeeded by one of his sons.

CA. 1074 B.C.—For safekeeping, Ramesses' mummy is moved from his plundered tomb. The body ends up in a secret tomb along with the remains of other New Kingdom pharaohs.

A.D. 1825—A British scholar discovers the tomb of Ramesses' sons, but the location is soon obscured by sand.

A.D. 1871—An Egyptian goatherder discovers the tomb containing Ramesses' remains.

A.D. 1886—Scholars unwrap Ramesses' mummy and examine his body.

A.D. 1904—Nefertari's tomb is found in the Valley of the Queens.

A.D. 1975—Ramesses' deteriorating body is taken to Paris and repaired.

A.D. 1985—The tomb of Ramesses' sons is rediscovered by an American scholar.

CHAPTER NOTES

CHAPTER 1. AN ENEMY TRAP

1. Kenneth A. Kitchen, *Ramesside Inscriptions*, vol. 2 (Oxford: Blackwell, 1996), p. 5.

2. Ibid., p. 4

3. Ibid., p. 15.

4. Ibid., pp. 15–16.

5. Ibid., p. 5.

6. Ibid.

CHAPTER 2. RISE TO THE THRONE

1. Lionel Casson, *Everyday Life in Ancient Egypt* (Baltimore: Johns Hopkins University Press, 2001), p. 5.

2. Ibid., p. 7.

3. James H. Breated, ed. and trans., *Ancient Records of Egypt*, vol. 3, (New York: Russell and Russell, 1962), pp. 113–114.

4. Kenneth A. Kitchen, *Ramesside Inscriptions*, vol. 2 (Oxford: Blackwell, 1996), p. 167.

5. Ibid.

6. Ibid., p. 168.

7. Ibid.

8. Ibid., p. 171.

9. Joyce Tyldesley, *Ramesses: Egypt's Greatest Pharaoh* (New York: Penguin, 2000), pp. 46–47.

CHAPTER 3. FAMILY AND PRIVATE LIFE

1. Gay Robins, *Women of Ancient Egypt* (Cambridge, Mass.: Harvard University Press, 1993), pp. 40–41.

2. Zahi A. Hawass, *The Mysteries of Abu Simbel: Ramesses II and the Temples of the Rising Sun* (Cairo, Egypt: American University in Cairo Press, 2001), p. 58

3. Kenneth A. Kitchen, *Pharaoh Triumphant: The Life and Times of Ramesses II* (Warminster: American University in Cairo Press, 1982), p. 85.

4. Terence Gray, *And in the Tomb Was Found, or Plays and Portraits of Old Egypt* (New York: D. Appleton, 1923), p. 56.

5. Joyce Tyldesley, *Ramesses: Egypt's Greatest Pharaoh* (New York: Penguin, 2000), p. 144.

CHAPTER 4. EARLY MILITARY EXPLOITS

1. Mark Healy, *The Warrior Pharaoh: Rameses II and the Battle of Qadesh* (Oxford: Osprey, 1993), p. 9

2. Ian Shaw, *Egyptian Warfare and Weapons* (Buckinghamshire, UK: Shire, 1991), pp. 49–50.

3. Kenneth A. Kitchen, *Ramesside Inscriptions,* vol. 2 (Oxford: Blackwell, 1996), p. 40.

4. Joyce Tyldesley, *Ramesses: Egypt's Greatest Pharaoh* (New York: Penguin, 2000), p. 67.

5. James H. Breasted, ed. and trans., *Ancient Records of Egypt*, vol. 3, (New York: Russell and Russell, 1962), p. 125.

6. Healy, p. 33.

7. Ibid., p. 27.

CHAPTER 5. RIVER OF BLOOD

1. Miriam Lichtheim, ed., *Ancient Egyptian Literature: A Book of Readings*, vol. 2 (Berkeley: University of California Press, 1975–1976), pp. 61–62.

2. Ibid., p. 62.

3. Ibid., p. 68.

4. Mark Healy, *The Warrior Pharaoh: Rameses II and the Battle of Qadesh* (Oxford: Osprey, 1993), p. 61.

5. Lichtheim, p. 66.

6. Healy, p. 76.

7. Lichtheim, p. 71.

8. Ibid., pp. 65–66.

9. Ibid., pp. 63, 71.

CHAPTER 6. MAKING PEACE

1. Trevor Bryce, *The Kingdom of the Hittites* (Oxford: Clarendon Press, 1998), p. 261.

2. Kenneth A. Kitchen, *Ramesside Inscriptions*, vol. 2 (Oxford: Blackwell, 1996), p. 46.

3. Kenneth A. Kitchen, *Pharaoh Triumphant: The Life and Times of Ramesses II* (Warminster: American University in Cairo Press, 1982), p. 69.

4. Bryce, p. 291.

5. Ibid., p. 310.

6. Ibid., p. 308.

7. Kitchen, *Ramesside Inscriptions*, p. 80.

8. Bryce, p. 306.

9. S. Langdon, and A.H. Gardiner, "The Treaty of Alliance Between Hattusilis, King of the Hittites, and the

Pharaoh Ramesses II of Egypt," trans. A.H. Gardiner, *Journal of Egyptian Archaeology*, vol. 6, 1920, p. 186.

10. Ibid.

11. Ibid., p. 187.

12. Ibid.

13. Ibid., p. 188.

14. Kitchen, *Pharaoh Triumphant*, p. 80.

15. Ibid., p. 69.

CHAPTER 7. A GREAT BUILDER

1. Zahi A. Hawass, *The Mysteries of Abu Simbel: Ramesses II and the Temples of the Rising Sun* (Cairo: American University in Cairo Press, 2001), pp. 44, 48.

2. Fabio Bourbon and Antonio Attini, *Egypt: Yesterday and Today* (New York: Stewart, Tabori, & Chang, 1981), p. 140.

3. D. B. Redford, "The Earliest Years of Ramessess II," *Journal of Egyptian Archaeology*, vol. 57, 1971, p. 113.

4. Percy Bysshe Shelley, "Ozymandias," first published January 11, 1818, in *The Examiner*, no. 524.

5. Joyce Tyldesley, *Ramesses: Egypt's Greatest Pharaoh* (New York: Penguin, 2000), p. 91.

6. Bernadette Menu, *Ramesses II: Greatest of the Pharaohs* (London: Harry N. Abrams, 1999), p. 77.

7. Kenneth A. Kitchen, *Pharaoh Triumphant: The Life and Times of Ramesses II* (Warminster: American University in Cairo Press, 1982), p. 20.

8. Ibid.

9. Hawass, pp. 69, 72, 76–77.

10. Kitchen, p. 136.

11. Ibid.

12. Gay Robins, *Egyptian Statues* (Buckinghamshire, UK: Shire, 2001), p. 7.

13. Mark Healy, *The Warrior Pharaoh: Rameses II and the Battle of Qadesh* (Oxford: Osprey, 1993), pp. 249–250.

14. Shelley.

CHAPTER 8. FINAL YEARS, DEATH, AND LEGACY

1. Kenneth A. Kitchen, *Pharaoh Triumphant: The Life and Times of Ramesses II* (Warminster: American University in Cairo Press, 1982), p. 206.

2. Ibid., p. 112.

3. Ibid., pp. 136–138.

4. Ibid., p. 214.

GLOSSARY

ASYLUM—Safety or refuge given by one person or group to another.

CANOPIC JAR—A container in which the ancient Egyptians placed the internal organs of a deceased person.

CARTOUCHE—An oval symbol containing the name or names of an Egyptian ruler.

COLOSSI—Giant statues.

CONSORT—The chief wife and queen of a male ruler.

DIADEM—A crown.

DYNASTY—A family line of rulers.

HOST—A modern term describing an ancient Egyptian army unit of five hundred men.

HYPOSTYLE HALL—A large chamber in which the ceiling is held up by columns spanning the room.

KHOPESH—A sword with a curved blade similar to a sickle's blade.

NATRON (OR NATRUM)—A mineral salt commonly used by the ancient Egyptians in the embalming process.

OBELISK—A tall, needle-shaped monument that in ancient Egypt usually stood in front of a temple.

PANTHEON—A group of gods worshiped by a people or nation.

PHARAOH—The king of ancient Egypt.

PYLON—A ceremonial gateway placed in front of an Egyptian temple.

REGNAL YEARS—The numbered years of a ruler's reign.

RELIEFS—Scenes carved into stone or plaster on walls or pillars.

SCRIBE—In the ancient world, an educated person who used reading and writing skills in his work.

SHOCK TACTICS—Direct, forceful contact made between the soldiers in opposing armies.

SISTRUM—An ancient Egyptian musical instrument that made a rattling sound.

SPHINX—A mythical creature having the body of a lion (or some other creature) and the head of a human.

STELE (PLURAL IS STELAE)—A stone or wooden slab, usually inscribed with words and/or scenes. Egyptian pharaohs often erected stelae to commemorate military campaigns and other achievements.

TRIBUTE—Money or valuables offered by one person or group to acknowledge the dominance of another.

FURTHER READING

BOOKS

Berger, Melvin and Gilda Berger. *Mummies of the Pharaohs: Exploring the Valley of the Kings*. Washington, D.C.: National Geographic Society, 2001.

Davis, Kenneth C. *Don't Know Much About Mummies*. New York: HarperCollins, 2005.

Hawass, Zahi. *Curse of the Pharaohs: My Adventures With Mummies*. Washington, D.C.: National Geographic Society, 2004.

Netzley, Patricia D. *The Greenhaven Encyclopedia of Ancient Egypt*. San Diego: Greenhaven Press, 2003.

Oakes, Lorna and Philip Steele. *Everyday Life in Ancient Egypt & Mesopotamia*. London: Southwater, 2005.

Perl, Lila. *The Ancient Egyptians*. New York: Franklin Watts, 2004.

Stefoff, Rebecca. *The Ancient New East*. New York: Benchmark Books, 2004.

Whiting, Jim. *The Life and Times of Ramses the Great*. Hockessin, Del.: Mitchell Lane Publishers, 2005.

Woods, Michael and Mary B. Woods. *Ancient Warfare: From Clubs to Catapults*. Minneapolis: Runestone Press, 2000.

INTERNET ADDRESSES

THE BATTLE OF KADESH

Read about one of the greatest battles of ancient times.
<http://www.reshafim.org.il/ad/egypt/>
Scroll down and click on the blue "battle of Kadesh" link.

EGYPTOLOGY ONLINE: RAMESSES II

This resource features several articles about the reign of Ramesses II and life in ancient Egypt.
<http://www.egyptologyonline.com/>
Click on "Egyptology Online" to enter site. Select "Pharaohs" at the left. Click on "Ramesses II."

INDEX